T0129175

HOW I MET
My *Spouse*

HOW I MET *My Spouse*

Twenty-Eight Short Stories

MIKE PAPPAS

HOW I MET MY SPOUSE
TWENTY-EIGHT SHORT STORIES

Copyright © 2017 Mike Pappas.

All rights reserved. No part of this book may be used or reproduced by any means, graphic, electronic, or mechanical, including photocopying, recording, taping or by any information storage retrieval system without the written permission of the author except in the case of brief quotations embodied in critical articles and reviews.

iUniverse books may be ordered through booksellers or by contacting:

iUniverse
1663 Liberty Drive
Bloomington, IN 47403
www.iuniverse.com
1-800-Authors (1-800-288-4677)

Because of the dynamic nature of the Internet, any web addresses or links contained in this book may have changed since publication and may no longer be valid. The views expressed in this work are solely those of the author and do not necessarily reflect the views of the publisher, and the publisher hereby disclaims any responsibility for them.

Any people depicted in stock imagery provided by Thinkstock are models, and such images are being used for illustrative purposes only. Certain stock imagery © Thinkstock.

ISBN: 978-1-5320-3000-0 (sc)
ISBN: 978-1-5320-3001-7 (e)

Library of Congress Control Number: 2017914721

Print information available on the last page.

iUniverse rev. date: 09/27/2017

A story of love, excitement, and humor!

I want to thank Anita Velantzas who inspired me to write this book!

The stories in this book are facts from friends and acquaintances. The format might be slightly altered to make the stories more exciting.

In some stories, names got edited.

CONTENTS

Shy one

My name is Angelo and was shy growing up, even in my late twenties remained shy.

My routine was the same get up to go to work, come home eat, read the newspaper and watch television.

While going to work, I see this girl. She was the most beautiful girl I have seen. It was love at first sight. How did I ever miss seeing her before!

I wanted so badly to say something but was just too shy.

Unfortunately, she exits the train before I ever got the nerve to say anything.

All day long she was on my mind. I never felt this way before, and it showed even my mother noticed my behavior and made a commit.

I was heartbroken when I did not see her and even waited a few minutes longer. It was getting late and had no choice but to leave for work.

After a week of not seeing her, I was upset and gave up realizing the girl of my dream was no longer. Then one morning while waiting for the train she appeared. She was walking right towards me.

Lost for words, and before I could even say a word, she disappears into the crowd.

I spotted her standing at the other end of the car. I tried fighting thru the crowd, but with no luck. By the time, I got even half way she was getting off. I was sorry I missed her, but at least she was back in the picture.

The next day I when I saw her, my heart started to beat fast, and again chicken out.

The next day I was determined to say something. I walked up to her and not wasting a second said, "Hello."

"I hope you do not think I'm nosy, but I did not see you last week."

She responds, "I was on vacation."

I introduce myself, and she says, "nice to meet you" and tells me her name is Collen.

Just saying hello made my day and I felt like a kid. I could not wait to see her again and hope I have the nerve to ask for her phone number.

It was time to make my move; it was now or never.

I asked her for her phone number, and she whispered it to me.

Getting connected

Now that I had her phone number, I was sort of nervous to call. Every time I dialed, not knowing what to say I hang up. Finally, after numerous attempts it started ringing; just as I'm ready to hang up, a voice says, "Hello."

With a crackle in my voice, I ask, "Is Collen there?"

"This is her mother may I ask who is calling."

I reply, "Angelo."

Her mother says, "I'm sorry she out, any message?" "No, just tell her I called."

I wanted so badly just to hear her voice, so after breakfast, I called. I could not sleep; I would toss and turn just thinking about her.

When she answers the phone, I was speechless for a moment.

"She says is that you Angelo!"

"Yes, it is I."

"My mother told me you called last night."

"I'm sorry I missed your call; I went out with my girlfriend."

I quickly say, "How about dinner, and a movie tonight." She says, okay. Great, "I'll pick you up at six."

First date

My mother questions me when she saw me shaving and showering late Saturday. I told her I have a date; my mom was happy knowing I was on the shy side.

On the way, I picked up some flowers. When I got to the front door, I could hear my heart beating loudly.

This little boy about seven or eight opens the door and says, "Are you my sister date." Their mother came and said, please come in and intrudes herself, "Colleen will be right out." Collen looked so beautiful as she walks into the room, I hand her the flowers.

Her father walks in and shakes my hand with a firm grip.

He says, "sit down" and asks me some questions.

After chatting a few minutes, Collen says, "we should get going." I say to myself "thank you," I was not ready to be interrogated just yet.

We dated a few months and felt she was the girl for me.

I told my mother I am going to ask her to go steady.

Mom said, "I hope you known what you are doing;" after all you only knew her for a short time. "Maybe you should date other girls!" I tried to explain with all my heart she is the girl for me.

I went to the jewelry store to pick out a friendship ring.

Bump in the road

I called Collen and told her I wanted to see her.

That night I ask her to go steady. She at first hesitated.

I said, "Do you not love me?"

"I do but my father is the problem, he could be very stubborn." I could sense she did not want to say the reason.

I replied, "is it because I am Italian."

She replies with shame in her voice, "yes my father is old fashion."

I tell her to take the ring, and hopefully, things will work out.

A few days later she called me to invite me for a Sunday dinner.

I told my mother, and she said just be you. I was kind of nervous not knowing how her father would react.

I stopped to get a bottle of wine and some desserts.

Her brother and sister answered the door, and the girl says, "my father does not like you."

Her mother hears her and says mind your manners, and apologized for her behavior.

When I walked into the living room their father was sitting watching football, he says, "sit do you like football?"

"Yes, I love the sport."

He shouts out to his wife, "bring us two beers." By halftime, we were talking like two old buddies.

We started having dinner, and he kept talking football. Finally, his wife says, "enough." Collen smiled when she sees how her father and I were getting acquainted.

Making it official

My company had season passes for the Giant home games, and I would get tickets on occasions. He was excited when I told him, and from that first game on we became a lot closer.

I asked Collen will you put the ring on now. She replies, "I am one step ahead of you," as she shows me her hand.

A few months later I told my parents that I'm going to ask Collen to marry me.

I spoke with her father about our intention, and he was happy to hear the good news.

I took her out for dinner and placed a small box next to her dessert. When she saw the box, she says, "what is this?" I say, "open it."

She started crying saying, "yes, yes."

After dinner, we went to her house first, then to mine to show them the ring.

Our families gave us an engagement party, and within a year we were married.

We moved to an apartment in the village.

We are proud parents of two boys and a girl.

Eye to eye

I came to New York to attend college and find a job that would fit into my school schedule.

Finally, after numerous attempts landed a job. I started working part-time at a men's department store as a cashier.

A lot of guys were always hitting on me, asking me for my phone number. I would use the excuse, "I cannot make conversation or write any message because of the security cameras." It seemed to work because they would stop asking.

One afternoon while working I looked up and noticed this huge fellow. He was nicely dressed wearing a suit and tie. I tried not to make it too obvious but our eyes caught each other. I would sneak another look and be hoping he would come to my register, but unfortunately, he went to another cashier. I felt bad as he was walking out the door.

A short time later he walks back in and again our eyes made connect. He wasted no time and came right to my register. He said you caught my eye and asked, "Do you have a boyfriend?" "I replied no, and why do you ask." He says, "may I have your phone number." I pointed to the security camera and said, "I cannot write anything." I said let me have your phone number, as I pulled out a register receipt and handed it to him.

He writes it down and says his name is, "Dave." What is your name? I said, "Mary." As he is leaving, he says, "don't forget to call."

I told my mother about him and what had happened. She says to be careful the world is a dangerous place, with a lot of crazy people and you cannot be careful enough.

I also told my girlfriend, and she said, "call him your 23 years old what do have to lose." I told her, "I have a pocketbook full of business cards from guys who tried to hit on me."

Dave most of thought I would never call him because for the first few days I was not even sure myself.

Getting together

Then I decided, he seemed like a good man, what do I have to lose.

I would leave a message on his answer machine; I hesitate to leave my phone number, so I just continue to call. Finally, after numerous attempts finally got to speak to him.

Remembering what my mother told me, we made plans to meet at a public location.

When I arrived, I walked right passed him. He had to call out my name to get my attention. I turn around and see this big huge stocky guy and say, "is that you Dave you look so different wearing street clothes."

We were seeing each other almost every weekend, and something always happened.

We were out this one night and noticed the car, was burglarized his golf clubs, and some of my belongings got stolen.

Another time while we were out for dinner we had a fender bender.

Meeting the parents

We had just returned from a date and parked in front of my apartment house. While we were saying goodnight, Dave shouts, "Oh my God that truck is not going to stop," as it slammed into our car. Our car hit the car in front of us and caused a chain reaction.

The accident was so loud many of the neighbors came out including my mother to see what happened. I called out to my mom, and she ran to look at how we were. My mother was all shaken up seeing the damaged cars.

When she saw, we were okay; I introduced Dave.

My uncle said to me, "you better stop seeing him this guy he seems to be bad luck."

We dated a few months and told me, "I want you to meet my parents."

I'll never forget the day I meet his parents. When we walked into the house, I must of track in some debris. His mother greeted us and followed me cleaning the floor where I walked. His father took a liking to me right away. Later his father told me secretly, that Dave was constantly talking about me.

Surprise, surprise

About a year later Dave was taking a business trip, and before he left, he stopped by to see me. While we were having lunch, I threw-up, and he remarks "are you all right you're not pregnant?"

I said, "a flat no."

Later that night I started feeling under the weather, so I purchased a pregnancy test only to discover I was pregnant.

Now I had to tell Dave; I had no idea how he would react, especially after telling him, "no."

When I told, him he remained speechless for a moment and muttered, "you're pregnant.".

When he got back from his meeting, he wasted no time and came to see me.

Maybe it was women's intuition, but I could sense he was pessimistic.

We still told no one and were planning on telling our parents together.

After we had told our parents, they seemed to be happy, not to mention shocked.

I went south to give birth where my other relatives lived.

We got blessed with a beautiful daughter that we named Sophia.

After giving birth, Dave came down to meet his new daughter and my relatives.

A short time later we came back and started our new life together.

Our parents were excited to meet their new granddaughter, especially his father.

Moving on

We started living together and made our residence in North Jersey. We could sense our parents were not too thrilled with the arrangements.

When Sophia turned a year old, we gave her a birthday party and invited family and friends.

A short time later we received bad news that Dave's father passed away. It was a difficult period for all of us, but like everything else, time heals all.

Two years later we decided to get married, being most of my family was down south we decided to get married there.

After the wedding, we came back home to start our new life together.

A few years later, we decided to buy a home and make our roots in central Jersey.

Years later we had another daughter we named Gaberlla.

Today we're blessed to have two beautiful daughters'.

$\mathcal{M}an,\ in\ blue$

My name is Carol I enjoyed traveling and made it a point every year to take a get- away vacation. I enjoyed going to Europe or one of the islands in the Caribbean. When I was not on vacation go to the Jersey shore on weekends; let's just say, "I love to party."

My family and friends would tell me to slow down and find a guy and settle down. I would just say yes, and continue my ventures.

I would date some of the local guys, but no one interests me.

So, I continued my Bachelorette lifestyle and was loving it.

My sisters had gotten married and would bug me to do the same. I say, "when I find Mr. right I'll do just that."

$Break\ in\ the\ action$

I worked for an insurance company and made friends with two of the girls. We became close friends and would have lunch together and see each other on weekends.

One of my girlfriends said, "I met this fellow named Lawrence he is a New York City police officer." "You both would make a lovely couple." It sounded exciting and said, "Do you think so."

My friend says let me give him your phone number and have him call you. I at first was a little reluctant to say yes. My other friend says, "go for it I met him and agreed you would make a beautiful couple."

I did not tell my parents anything just yet, just in case, it did not work out.

A few days later he called me, and we spoke briefly.

Lawrence would call me regular, and kept in contact by phone for a few months.

My parents got wind of it and were curious about him, but I wouldn't say much.

First date

Lawrence called only this time ask if I would like to go to the mountains with a few other couples and spend the weekend. I first hesitated, then happily say, "why not."

Even though we were phone buddies for the last few months, this would be the first time we would see each other and physical meet.

I still did not tell my parents anything yet. I would just say that I was going to spend the weekend with my friends, and just wait till after our first date.

We had a great time together and felt it was time for Lawrence to meet my parents.

So, I invited him for a Sunday dinner.

I was a little edgy not knowing how it would turn out. Lawrence seemed calm and relaxed. I was happy my parents took a liking to him from day one, especially my dad. In fact, they hit it off well my dad started treated him more like his son.

Getting serious

We continued dating and could sense he was getting serious. After dating five months, he says let's go downtown to the jewelry exchange to look at some rings. I somehow knew we were going to get engaged, but hearing him say that I got excited. It was then I realized he was the guy for me.

I had an idea the kind of diamond I wanted, after trying different types fell in love with this oval ring shape ring. The jeweler handed Lawrence the box, and he opens it and says, "put it on." With Christmas coming soon, I said no, "give to me on Christmas day."

He opens it again, and I said, "not now."

Lawrence started to tease me and continued, to open the box. Finally, after doing it numerous times, I broke down. The ring looked so much more beautiful when he put it on my finger. I decided to leave it on.

We were both so excited we had to show it to our family's. They were so happy and overjoyed they gave us an engagement party a few weeks later.

We were married shortly later.

We moved to Staten Island, and years later we made our roots in New Jersey.

Today we have two wonderful sons and two beautiful grandchildren.

4

Super meet

My name is Carol, I was in my early 40's and had my share with some bad experience. I was laid back in rushing to meet any guys. I was even engaged, and that left me with a bad taste.

Working during the week was tough, so I could only find time do my food shopping on weekends.

This one Saturday while shopping I had this gut feeling that someone was stalking me. While at the meat department digging looking for the smallest steak being it was just for me. This fellow started making a remark to me. At first, I thought he worked there because I was making a mess looking for the steak.

I started to straighten out the meats that I messed up and then realized he was also just a customer. He started making conversation and says, "you have a beautiful smile." I thank him and continued shopping.

While reaching for an item on the shelf, he appears and says," Hello" again. He caught me off guard and said, "for someone as young and beautiful as you, are you married you can't be single?"

I say, "yes I am single."

He introduced himself and told me his name, "Gerard." I say my name, and again says, "I can't believe you are not married." He tells me he was also single, but divorced with three sons. We spoke for a few minutes and asked me for my number. At first, I was a little reluctant, thinking back to all the bad luck I had an encounter.

He said his cell phone was in for repair. He seemed very friendly and sincere, so I gave him my phone number and my e-mail address.

First date and beyond

We started to e-mail each other on a regular basis.

When he regained his phone back, we began chatting every few days. He later asked me for a date and agreed to meet him.

We dated a few weeks, and he says, "I still cannot believe you are not involved with anyone."

My birthday was coming, and Gerard took me out to celebrate. While we were having dinner, he proposed to me. I immediately said, "slow down cowboy we just met." He tried to convince me but just brushed off the idea.

He asked to see me again next week, and I accepted, I was still shocked that he proposed to me so soon.

On our next date, again while we had some cocktails he again asks me to get married. I said, "hold on what is the rush we are still getting to get to known each other." I could sense he was disappointed that I said, "No."

I just felt we had just met and starting to enjoy each other's company.

We made plans to see each other the following weekend.

My life changes

I told my family about Gerard, and there were mixed emotions. My friends were all happy for me.

I enjoyed his company; he had a pleasant personality and a great sense of humor.

Whenever we were together, I was always happy and content.

Even though we only knew each other for a short time I wanted my family to meet him. So, I invited Gerard for dinner; they all like him and his sense of humor.

I met his family and took a liken to his three sons.

We continued seeing each other on a regular basis.

Call it a women's intuition; this one time I wanted to look even nicer, so I went and had my hair done and even purchased a new dress.

While we were having dinner, I could sense he was going to ask me again. My intuition was right on while we had dessert he says, "let's get married." I happily say okay; I must have caught me off guard because I said, "Yes." He gives me a huge hug and kisses me.

Without wasting any time, we go to this local jewelry store to pick out a diamond ring.

Everything was happening so fast. I haven't felt this excited and happy since I can't remember when.

I could not wait to tell everyone the exciting news.

My family and friends were happy for me.

We had a small wedding and decided to move to South Carolina and start our new life together and make it our new home.

Second chance

My name is Donna, I was in my early thirty's and was reasonably attractive, I stood 5' 5 and had an excellent shape. I just came out of a bad marriage and kept a low profile. As much as I wanted children, I was glad we never had any.

My parents ask me if I wanted to move back home after my break up. I enjoyed my independence and told them not to worry.

After a few months, I started going out and was trying to find Mr. Right. I would go to some of the local clubs. All the guys I encountered only had one thing on their minds, "Sex."

A different approach

My problem was all my friends were married with children; so, basically had no choice but to go alone.

So, after a few weeks of laying back, I decided to try something different like a dating club. I started to e-mail this fellow Michael, and from what he said we had a lot in common. After a few weeks of corresponding, we made plans to meet at a public location.

He greeted me with a kiss on my cheek. He was even better looking than I even hoped. He says, "I trust you're hungry; I know an excellent restaurant." We chatted well into the night that they had to chase us out. He took me home and gave him my phone number and made a date for the following weekend.

I had mixed emotions but realized maybe I was just being over cautious coming out of a bad marriage.

Drastic change

We started seeing each other almost every weekend, going to the movies and Broadway shows. I was starting to have deep feelings for Michael.

Then it happened he told me he was in the Army reserve and his unit was activated and being sent to Iraq.

I wanted him to meet my parents before his deployment, so I invited him for dinner. He brought a bottle of wine and flowers that made my mother's eyes sprinkle. My parents took a real liking to Michael.

We spent more time together, not knowing how long he would be gone.

I'll never forget the day we said goodbye even though we only knew each other a few months. I felt like something inside of me was missing.

He gave me a friendship ring and said, "when he returns he will exchange it for a diamond ring."

Lonesome

It was hard at first trying to adjust; it was a feeling I never experienced before. I would take one day at a time.

Every time I listen to the news about soldiers getting injured or killed a piece of me would die. It got to the point I did not want to hear the news.

A few weeks later I received a letter from Michael, that would heal that part of me. I would read it repeatedly. I write Michael almost every day. It gave me a warm feeling that he was not far away.

I received a letter that just ate me up; his platoon had gotten hit by a rocket attack that killed a few of his friends. He and others were lucky only to receive minor injuries.

Coming home

After a long, long 18 months of loneliness, he wrote saying he was coming back. It felt like my other half came to life.

When Michael arrived, we spent the next few days together. I felt like a new person.

He wasted no time saying, "remember what I told you when I left!" We went down to the jewelry exchange and picked out the diamond ring he had promised me.

We went straight home to show my parents. My family was so excited about getting engaged they threw us a big engagement party a few weeks later.

Michael told me when he went to his old job they refused to hire him back. They claimed he was absent too long to hold his job. He had worked as an auto mechanic for this car dealership for over three years.

He was not one to make a big scene about it and just put it behind him and went job hunting.

After a few interviews, he got a better offer, making more money.

While having dinner, my father bought up the subject about his previous company. My dad was furious that they refused to hire him back especially after spending eighteen months defending our country.

A few days later, he told Michael, his friend who is a lawyer told him the whole story. He said you have a good case against them. We spoke about it, and he decided to proceed with the lawsuit and let the system work it out.

Satisfaction

We started making plans for our wedding only to discover that the church would not allow me to be married because of being divorced. I wanted a church wedding, so I did not know what to do. My mother says to me what don't you go to the Protestant church and see if they will marry you.

I told Michael about the idea and said okay. So, we went and spoke with the minister and gave us our blessings and we set a date.

We were married six months later and spent our honeymoon at St. Thomas.

When we got back home, we lived in my apartment.

We planned on having a family and buying a home.

Three years later we were blessed with a daughter.

More good news, Michael received a settlement for his past job that denied him. He received enough for a down payment for our dream home.

Within six months we moved into our new home.

Today we live in suburban Maryland and have three beautiful daughters.

High school sweethearts

My name is Yvonne and was a junior in high school and a plain Jane. In fact, many of my classmates would call him a dork. I must admit they were somehow correct. So, to overcome this downfall, I make it up by being very forward and speak my mind.

I had a crush on this Slovakia fellow nickname Peppy from the neighborhood. He was tall and incredibly handsome. Peppy played on the high school basketball team, and I went to every game just to watch him play.

Our school was having a Sadie Hawkins dance, and I wanted so badly to go with him. Unfortunately, he was going with another girl. I did not know what to do because I wanted so badly to see him. I decide to go with some of the girls from the neighborhood.

When we arrived, Eddy was dancing, and I do anything to be able to dance with him. Eddy's date went into the bathroom, and I approached her and asked, "Do you mind if I dance with Eddy?" She replies sarcastically, "go ahead I don't care."

Without wasting a minute, walked up to Eddy and said, "I spoke with your friend Maria and asked her if we could dance, and told me she did not mind." Eddy smiles and says, "okay with me."

When she returned, she wasn't a happy camper and storms off. After we finish that dance, we continued to dance the night away. At the end of the dance, Eddy took me home.

Getting involved

We saw each other quite often, and a lot of the girls would say, "how did you ever hook up with him, he is so good looking, and you are a dork." I would just say, "I 'don't know, maybe God put us together." We were total opposites; he was very passive and laid back and sweet, and I was forward, and he liked that.

I'll never forget we enjoyed dancing so much, we entered a dance contest and won. My curfew was midnight, but because of the competition, I was late getting home. Eddy dropped me off; knowing I was late, tried sneaking in but my mother was up and waiting to scold me. Mom shouts, "young lady, do you realize what time it is." I apologized and showed her the trophy we won, and she felt bad after explaining the circumstances.

Getting serious

When we were in high school, our parents did not give it a second thought when we saw each other. Years later after school, we were still dating. We were seriously starting to talk about marriage. His mother was not too thrilled because I was Italian and she wanted Eddy to marry a Slovakia girl.

My mom was happy and surprise because she loved Eddy. His mother eventually came around, and we started making wedding plans. The wedding turned out just as we were hoping and our parents were happy.

After we returned from our honeymoon, we live close to my family.

Our new life

When we discovered we could not have children of our own we decided to adopt. We were blessed to adopt a boy, and two years later we adopt another boy.

Remembering what the priest had told us, "what you get married for, you can also divorce for."

We at first thought our children were the problem when our marriage was on shaky grounds. We both loved each other and decided to go and seek a marriage counselor and try and work it out. It was then we realized my being forward and his laid-back attitude was causing our life together to have its problems.

We would go religiously for counseling, finally, after four years we found ourselves even more loving. So, I thank God it all worked out, which brought us closer as well as our families.

Our Life takes a turn

I was always a believe whatever happens in life, happens for a reason. After our counseling, my feeling started to take a different approach to my life and began to feel charismatic with my church. I got more involved in my new church belief and would attend the charismatic masses. It was a new feeling I never experience till now. At the mass, I found the music different; it was hot-warming, breathtaking and beautiful. At one of the masses I saw Jesus, it was not that I saw Him, but I felt His presence. At that moment, I felt He loved us.

Now that Jesus came into our lives, our marriage became ever stronger!

Getting what you want

My name is Anita shortly after graduating got a full-time job and went to live on my own. I met a lot of single girls and guy's whom also lived in the same complex.

I became friends with some of the girls, and we would hang out on weekends at a place called Salisbury beach.

This one Saturday a few of my new girlfriends and I went to this beach party where there were a lot of single guys.

One of my friends says to me see that tall, thin fellow; his name is Jim. He works for the same company as you. She says let me introduce him.

When she introduces us, we were both wearing our bathing suits and started making a chic chat. I told Jim that I had a kink in my neck and before I knew it he was giving me a back rub; it was love at first touch. We seemed to hit it off, we spoke about things in general.

I told my friend, "I am going to marry that fellow, Jim!" My friend laughed and said, "good luck."

First try

Whenever I went upstairs where Jim worked, I'd see him. We chat a while and have a few laughs. He asked me for my phone number and said he would call me and make plans to go out. I got all excited that he asks me for my phone number.

A whole month pass and no phone call so I was kind of upset. Being we worked for the same company I was looking forward to seeing Jim again; I had to go upstairs to make copies and was hoping to run into him.

While using, the copy machine he comes behind me and says hello. I just melted when I saw him. He says do you want to go out; I got so excited I had to hold back my emotions. Two weeks pass and again no phone call or anything, again I was upset.

I was upstairs doing some paperwork and spot him and say hello, he acted as nothing happen. He says hi, and says" please sit." We chatted about work and said how about going out. Under my breath, I'm saying, "that son of a bitch, I have been waiting all this time."

Jim finally called me and made plans for dinner. I was so excited that we were finally going to go on a real date.

We had such a great time together and was so impressed. Jim was such a gentleman and fun to be together.

Now I was convinced I was going to marry Jim.

After he dropped me off he says, "let's redo it, I'll call you." One week goes by, still not a phone call.

Change of pace

After not hearing from him for a few weeks, and not even seeing him I just wanted to hear his voice. I did want to show him I was forward, so decided to call him.

I dialed his number, and he answers, "Hello." He kept repeating, "Hello, hello anybody there." I was so happy just to hear his voice, and that made my day.

A few days later I ran into him at work, and we started talking, and he said, "I meant to call you, but something always came up."

He called a few days later, and we made plans to go out. We started seeing each other more often.

I do anything for Jim, when he asks me to stop smoking because it was not healthy, I did.

After a few dates, he says, "I want you to be my girl," and we started going steady. I was the happiest girl in the world.

At first, I thought being we were going steady we would see other two to three times a week. It turned out we were seeing each other once a week.

Getting serious

For all the time, we saw each other we still did not meet each other's, parents. When my parents had questioned me, I would say that we were just dating.

After we had dated a few months, we were talking about marriage. Jim wanted to wait three years. I was not thrilled and say, "that's too long." We would go back and forth I said, "let's wait two years," and he agreed.

He asked me if I wanted an engagement ring; I had the impression he could not afford it. He was driving an old beat-up car and just thought he was too poor to buy a ring. So, I just said, "no it's not necessary." I just felt having him, "a ring was not essential!"

So, we made it official and got engaged without a ring. He repeated it again, "are you sure!" Just to known, we would be married the ring was not significant.

Meeting the parents

Jim felt it was time for me to meet his parents, and what a better way to tell them the good news. I was not sure how his parents would take to me. He was Greek, and I was Italian.

The Greek Easter was coming up and invited my parents and me to join his family to celebrate their Easter. I was nervous hoping to win his parents over.

He told me not to worry his parents were not old fashion, where he had to just married a Greek girl. That made me feel a little more relaxed but kept my guard up.

When we told our parents the news, they were happy as could be.

His parents took a liking to me and that made things a lot easier as we moved closer to our marriage. His father treated me like part of the family. Both our parents became close, and we were happy for that.

The big day

We started talking more in detail about the wedding; was it going to be a small or a large wedding and of course our parents would speak their mind.

Our parents were not financially capable of paying for the wedding, but Jim made it clear that he would take care of the expenses.

I was so happy when I think back it was just five years ago when we first met and had said to my friends, "I was going to marry him."

The wedding went over with no problems, even the reception as big as it was.

Oh, well I guess we did have a little excitement. Near the end the singer that we engaged passed out. I guess when you have an open bar anything is possible.

After the reception, we changed into our street clothes and jumped into Jim's car to start our honeymoon. We were going to drive up to Canada. As we are driving the cars starts to make a spitting sound and goes dead. Here we are in the middle of nowhere, and Jim shouts out, "with all the excitement I forgot to fill the gas tank."

We get out of the car, and there was no one around, it was total darkness except for the stars from above. We walk down the road and see this run down seeded motel that look like a horror movie set.

All I thought what a way to spend our honeymoon, we had no choice but to check in and hope for the best. Being it was our honeymoon nothing was going to ruin it.

The next morning, we got the tank filled and continued our trip and had a beautiful honeymoon.

Never too late

When we got back home, we got an apartment downstairs from his parents in a town outside of Lowell Mass.

Years later Jim surprise me with the most beautiful diamond ring. He apologized and said, "I'm sorry I never gave you this when we first got engaged." He placed it my figure and gave me a hug.

Today we have two sons and a daughter and five grandchildren.

Blind date

My name is Marion; it was just my older sister and me. We had just moved from Manhattan to Queens. Our father saw the neighborhood was changing and not for the better. I was in my teens and was going to miss a few of my friends, and most likely never see them again.

I started attending a church youth club where I meet others my age; I became close to one of the girls.

My new friends say, "I met this guy and felt he would be a good match for you."

I say, "what's the catch?"

She hesitates and says, "I have good and bad news."

What's the good news, "he is a good guy and comes from a lovely family?"

Without wasting another second, I say, "what's the bad news?"

"He is Italian."

I ask her, "what his name?"

She replies, "Vincent."

I was lost for words, knowing how my family might react.

For the next few days, I was debating if I should chance the idea. What's the worst that could happen, "my father kills me?"

Taking a chance

I thought it out and decided to meet him and just keep it a secret from my parents.

So, I tell my friend, "okay set up the date." My friend made plans to meet in the city. Thinking, being far from home nobody would be any wiser. I was kind of nervous; this was my first time doing something like this.

I met Vincent at this restaurant where we had lunch. I was delighted he was just as my friend said, "a pleasant, nice guy and friendly."

We made plans to see each other the following weekend. I felt guilty doing this so told my parents a little white lie; I was going out with my girlfriend. Even though he had my phone number, he knew he could not call me.

We went to this quiet place, and have a few drinks. Then Vincent started getting a little fresh; I guess I spoke too soon, he was friendly all right. Too familiar for me, so I cut him short and stopped seeing him.

Time heals all

About a year later Vincent calls; I was just starting to forget him. I was speechless for words and a little hesitant at first to talk to him. He apologized for the way he had acted the last time we saw each other.

Being a mercenary person, "I forgave him."

He told me he just purchased a new car and was going into the Army Reserves in a few weeks and would be back in six months after all his training.

So, we saw each other quite a bit before he left for active duty.

Vincent said, "what about us getting married when he returns from active duty." I was a little reluctant, especially with my parents and said, "let's see what happens when you return."

Somehow my parents got wind of us seeing each other. My mother was not to thrill. My father would ignore it and felt once he was in the service it would all be history.

My parents wanted us to marry a Greek boy and have a family. So, for that reason, I would never dream to bring him to my house.

We would write each other and could sense my parents were not very happy.

I would try to avoid them seeing Vincent's mail, but occasionally one would sneak through.

Wedding bells

Vincent was due home within a few days and remember what he said about getting married. No sooner he was home the first thing Vincent asks, "Are we getting married?" While he was, away I was tormenting the idea about getting married; so, I told him, "yes."

He looked like he was shocked that I said, "yes."

Vincent wasted no time, and we went to look at engagement rings.

Now that I told Vincent okay; I had to tell my parents the news about getting engaged.

That night I showed my parents the ring. My father looks at it and says, "anybody whom could afford to buy a ring like this I have to meet."

When my dad made that remark, I had a smile a mile long.

My mother's birthday was coming up and ask her, "what do you want for your birthday?"

She replies, "please invite Vincent over for a Sunday dinner." That would be a perfect gift and make me happy.

So, I called Vincent and told him.

He said, "you mean your family was not upset."

I told him, "let's take it one step at a time."

We were both nervous not knowing how it would play out. After dinner, we wait into the parlor, and my father wasted no time telling him; "I have but one request, that you get married in our faith, Greek Orthodox."

Vincent being a gentleman agreed.

We chatted a little about the wedding; my mother wasted no time, and we started making the arrangements for our big day.

To save time if you saw the movie "My Big Fat Greek Wedding" the first one, that says it all.

Pleasing my parents

When I gave birth to a boy, my parents were so excited especially my father, having daughters. It was more than my parents could have wanted. He had all the features a grandfather could wish a blue-eyed blond. Just like my dad when he was a child.

We later moved to South Carolina, and today we have a son and daughter, three grandchildren and five great-grandchildren.

What more could I wanted!

9

Getting it right

M y name is Milt and just returned from what seemed like was a lifetime tour of duty in Korea. Everything had gone well, except just one thing before coming home I was a victim of a Dear John.

It left a bitter taste in my mouth, so I just kept a low profile on dating.

To keep busy socially, I go to one of the local bar's in my neighborhood and reunite with the old gang, who was still around. A lot of the guys were married; and unfortunately, some killed during the war.

Between my family and friends, they would encourage me to start dating again.

Getting back into my routine

I started going back to my church. I would meet some of the old crowd and some new friends. I ran into an old friend Maria whom I haven't seen since being back. We spoke about my bad experience and was understanding and said, "I'm sure you will meet the right girl."

I told her that I was having no luck finding the right girl. Maria responds I known just the girl for you. I teased her and said, "whom, you."

"No, no, my sister."

You have a sister, "how come I never met her before."

She is not a churchgoer and does not get involved with the church activities. Maria told me her name was Karen and a little about her, and she sounded interesting.

So, I told her, "fix me up."

Learning experiences

Maria called me and said, "it's set up." I was to meet her Saturday. I felt kind of funny; this was my first time going on a blind date even though I knew her sister.

I purchased a box of chocolates and flowers. I was a little nervous when ringing the doorbell. Maria answers the doors and says, "come in Karen will be right here." Her parents were both there, and she introduces me.

Karen comes into the room, and she looked just as her sister described her. I hand her the flowers and candy. She thanks me, and says, "let's go."

She asks, "where are we going?"

I say, "dinner and a movie."

She says, "I rather we did not go to a movie."

"So, what would you like to do?"

"Let's go to a club."

After dinner, we went to this club she recommended.

The waitress says hello to Karen by her first name.

I say, "I guess she knows you."

Without hesitating says, "yes."

We order drinks, and she says, "let's dance." I enjoyed dancing, and that seemed to please her.

After a few dances, I say, "let us sit for a while." She says, "just one more," and before I knew, we were dancing continuously. I said that it for me and started walking back to the table and she continued dancing.

She shouts come on, "I'm just warming up."

She finally realizes I was not giving in and comes back to the table.

We were making conversation, and this fellow comes up to the tables and asks her to dance. She starts to get up to dance, and I put up my hand and say, "excuse me, but she is with me." He gives me a dirty look and walks off.

I tell her, "you were going to dance with him, knowing you can with me?

She says, "why not, is there anything wrong with that?"

Not to start any argument, I just ignored her commit.

As we are going home, she says, "I hope you are not mad at me."

I said no, "I guess you love to dance."

She smiles and says, "I could dance all night."

I dropped her off, and she gives me a kiss, and says "thanks for a fun evening."

Getting to know you

We dated a few months and was getting to fall for Karen. Was it because I was on a rebound after my bad experience.

Whenever I pick Karen up from the house, her sister Maria was always there. She would tease me while waiting for Karen.

A short time later I was beginning to see a change and realizing that Karen was drifting away.

So, I just came out and said, "is there anything wrong?"

She says, "as a matter of fact there is."

"Don't get upset but I rather we stop seeing each other!"

My first reaction was, "I did something wrong?"

She says no, "it's not you; it's I."

I took her home and became very depressed.

Was it me, first a Dear John, and now this.

Right under my nose

While I was at the church, I ran into Maria, and she was sorry about what happened with her sister. "I told her it's water under the bridge, how about we go and grab a bit to eat."

It's funny I've known Maria for years and never look at her but just a friend. It was not till now; I realized how much we had in common. We spent over two hours just talking. I told Maria I would love to see her again; she felt funny because of the circumstances. I suggested we just meet somewhere.

We started seeing each other and told no one. This one night when we said goodnight, I kissed her. Before I had a chance to apologized for kissing her, Maria in return kisses me.

We kissed again, and Maria whispers in my ear, "I love you."

I realized then she was my missing link in life.

I said, "what do we do now?"

Maria says, "we just tell everyone."

"What about your sister."

I know my sister, "everything will be all right."

Happy, happy

We made plans to tell our families first hers, then mine.

29

We told her family that we had some happy and exciting news.

I'll never forget the expression Karen gave when she saw us together and holding hands.

We told them the good news that we are getting engaged and planning for the big day within the year. Her parents were so happy when we told them they embraced us.

Her sister finally after getting over the shock says, "when did this all happen?" She congratulates us with a hug.

My family was also shock and excited.

Both our parents gave us an engagement party, and we set a date for our wedding

Everything went well; her sister was the maid of honor.

Her parents went all out and gave us a real elegant wedding.

I realized now sometimes the things you are looking for, "are right under your nose."

Today we have three beautiful daughters and five grandchildren.

Down on the Farm

M y name is Lee after I had turned eighteen decided to move from the big city hassle, and relocate up to the Catskill mountains to live with my grandmother. My parents were not too thrilled especially my mother and would try to talk me out of going.

When I graduated high school, I wanted to enjoy the summer before starting to look for a job. I remember going to the Catskill while I was growing up with my parents for our summer vacation. So, I knew a little about the area.

Landing a job

The summer flew by, and it was time to start job hunting. The few dollars that I saved were starting to deplete. I had no choice knowing without enough money I just could afford to buy a car, so I had to use grandma car.

They were hiring at this paper factory in a town called Kingston it was about thirty miles from the house. So, I put on my only white shirt and tie and went job hunting.

They gave me a pre-application form to fill out. After filling out the form, would call me in for an interview and be sure to bring all proper IDs.

As I was heading home noticed a sign saying, "construction help needed."

So, I decided to check it out. I had nothing to lose, and drove a few miles down the road and came to this construction site. I went inside and spoke with this big huge guy, and told him about the sign that you were looking for help. He asks me all kinds of questions; I guess he liked my answers and said the job was mine. He gave me all the details and told me to fill out some papers in the office.

I thanked him and went into the room where this cute girl was working. I told her the man next door ask me to fill out some applications.

As I was filling out this one form, it wanted a social security number. I had no such number, so I tell the girl, and she says without that we cannot hire you. She told me I had to go a social security office to apply.

Help

I started heading back home, after applying for my social security. The car started spitting and jerking and went dead. Here I am on this deserted road, and it was beginning to get dark. Thank God, I could hear a car coming and flagged it down, much to my surprise it was that cute girl from the office.

She says, "what happened?"

I told her the car just died.

"Are you out of gas," she says.

Feeling like an idiot said, "oh boy you know you might be right."

She drove me to a local gas station to get some gas and drove me back. She waited to make sure the car started. Now for sure, I felt like a real idiot when it started.

I thanked her and said, "I like to make this up to you."

She says, "I'm sure we can work something out."

Making contact

I decided to take the job at the paper mill, once my social security card arrived I started working.

I called the construction site and told him and was very understanding.

I started my new job and decided to treat myself to lunch, knowing if I wanted to save money had to start brown bagging my lunch.

So, I went to this local restaurant and ran into the cute girl that came to my rescue. I said, "nice to see you again, may I join you." After all this, I do not even remember your name. She tells me her name is, "Donna," and before she left I ask to see her again. We had made a date for the following weekend.

I met her parents and did not realize that tall guy from the construction site was her father. He had remembered me from the previous meeting and ask me about my new job.

Making our move

We dated for over a year and wanted to get married. The problem was we did not have much money saved.

Her father told us we could live in the guest house until we felt comfortable financially.

When I told my family, and friends the news, there were mixed emotions.

We were too young.

We were not financially fit.

We just met.

We were tired of hearing all the negatives and decided to make a move.

We told both our parents what our plans were and her parents were all in. My parents were just the opposite.

Her parents suggested having the wedding right here on the farm. So, we planned a summer wedding. We had a large wedding over 100 people. We couldn't ask for a better day; the weather was picture perfect.

Her parents paid for the wedding and even gave us a honeymoon gift to St. Thomas.

We spent the next few years living with her parents and living the farm life, which got into my blood.

So, we decided to buy a farm ourselves. We purchased a small farm about thirty miles north of her parents.

We recently celebrated our Fifty anniversary.

Today we have three sons, six grandchildren, and two great-granddaughters.

This side of Heaven

My name is Ann and was born and raised up in the Bronx New York and lived with my brother and sister.

Our cousin was graduating from the Greek Orthodox seminary, and we all went to celebrate his new life in the priesthood. After the ceremony, we congratulate him and later were going to his home for a celebration party.

I met a friend of mine who was also at the ceremony and introduced me to a friend of hers, and we started making conversation.

His name was John and was very talkative, and we chatted for quite a while. It was getting late, and I had to meet up with my family so cut him short and left.

It wasn't till later I realized he must be thinking the worse of me. Oh, well what were the odds we see each other again.

You never know

I enjoyed going to the Greek festivals with my family, or sometimes I go with my girlfriends.

This one time I had gone, with my family I heard someone calling my name. I turn around, and it is that fellow John that I met a few months ago, at my cousin graduation. He says, "what happened that day you left so fast I did have a chance to say goodbye, you just brush me off." "Oh no, I'm sorry I explained that I had to rush to meet my family that day."

I told my family I was going to spend some time with a friend. My father made a commit about it. I replied, he was someone I met at our cousin's ceremony a few months ago. He wasn't too thrilled and told me not to be long.

I met up with John, and we started chatting and asked me if I wanted something to eat. I had to cut him short again and said," thank you but no."

John asked to see me again and asks for my phone number.

John called a few days later and made a date, and we started seeing each other more often.

My father questions me about John.

I told my parents that they would meet him shortly.

We started seeing each other almost every weekend.

I could sense John was getting serious, so I just took one day at a time.

I was also falling for John, and he was very frank and family-oriented.

After meeting John, my parents took a liking to him, especially my father.

One step closer

John told me he was entering the priesthood and ask my hand in marriage.

I liked John but was not sure how I would fit into this lifestyle. We spoke about it and decided to tell our parents.

When I told my parents, my father was reluctant at first. My mother loved John and was happy with the marriage and gave her blessings.

My father eventually came around and gave us his blessings.

We got engaged, soon after and were married before John graduated from the ministry.

John was assigned to a church in the south and made it our new home.

Today we have five beautiful children.

Two times a charm

My name is Jock and grew up in New York City. My parents migrated from Spain in the early 40's.

At the ripe age of seventeen, I met this girl named Tina who was from the neighborhood. The problem was she was Greek, and her parents were old fashion. We kept it hush, but living so close to each other made it that much more challenging.

My parents were down to earth and understanding, so on my end, there was no problem. On the other side of the coin, her parents were very strict and wanted her only to get involved with Greek boys.

Her family attended a Greek church in our neighborhood. Tina belonged to the churches youth club. We would use this as an excuse to get together and keep her parents from getting suspicious.

My sister and I were very close, so I told her about the situation. She said, "just tell her parents." I responded, "maybe her father, as for her mother forget it."

We continued to manage to avoid her parents from finding out, which was no small task.

A slight separation

The Korea war had just broken out and soon after received a letter from Uncle Sam welcoming me.

I had thirty days before leaving for basic training.

My parents took it bad. Now I had to tell Tina and knew she was not going to like the news. Sure, enough she broke down and started crying.

I got stationed at Fort Dix in New Jersey, which was only a couple of hours away.

After eight weeks of basic training received a week of leave before starting advanced training.

Not realizing we let our guard down and her family found out, that we saw each other. Her mother was all over Tina to stop seeing me. At this point, we could care less.

The week flew by and was back for my advanced training which was another eight weeks. At the end of my training received my new assignment and it was not good news. I did not know how to tell Tina, because as bad as I felt she would take it that much worse.

When I told her, the bad news going to Korea, she broke down and started crying. I said, "let's get married."

She stops crying and says, "are you for real."

I say, "Let's elope."

Within a week, we went and had our blood work and were soon married by the justice of the peace down at city hall.

We told no one except my sister and asked her to keep it quiet till I get back from my tour of duty in Korea.

She told her parents she was going to spend the night at her friend's house so that we could have at least one night together before my thirteen-month tour of duty.

We would write each other; the problem was her mother would sometimes discard some of my letters. So, I would send them to my sister to avoid this from happening.

As the months were passing, we knew we had to tell our parents, with my parents I did not see a problem. Our concern was her parents, especially her mother.

Breaking the news

When I got home, we now had to tell our parents the shocking news.

We decided to tell my parents first and save the shocker for last. My family was jubilant for us and wanted to help us get our new life started. We knew telling her parents would not be as easy, but it had no choice.

We waited for Sunday after her parents came home from church to give them the news. When her mother saw, me she started talking in Greek and from the tone I knew it was not pleasant.

Tina said, "we have something to tell you."

She says to her parents in Greek, "we are married."

There is a period of quietness; then her mother screams out with anger in her voice. Even though it was in Greek, I could sense the bitterest in her voice. She started doing the sign of the cross and was going on and on; her father tries to calm her down but with no luck.

Her brother walks in and says, "what's going on I could hear mom from outside?" Her brother recognized me from the church group. Tina explained everything and says, "congratulations."

Her mother finally calms down but not for long. She started ramming some broken English and goes on and on. Tina spoke to her but to no prevail, all she kept shouting was "divorce, divorce," in her broken English.

There was quietness for a short period and starts up again; Her father says, "enough they are married, not that I agree with this type of arrangement."

We will discuss more in detail later when things calm down.

I still had a few months before being discharged from active service.

Tina stayed with her family until being discharged.

I told her privately, "start looking for an apartment."

Trying to please everyone

When I came home Tina had the apartment ready; the funny part was her mother even help pick out some of the furniture. She told me her mother suggest we get separate beds; I told her I don't think so.

Tina was working full time earning a decent salary. I had saved most of my money from the army.

Her parents wanted to talk to us regarding our marriage. They wanted us to be re-married in a Greek Orthodox church.

It did not stop there; they also wanted me to convert. I loved Tina and would do anything to make her happy. When I told my family, their response was, "whatever makes you happy."

They knew the circumstances and were very supported.

I started attending classes learning the Orthodox religion. When I completed the education part, I was to be baptism before we were married. I did not know anyone, so I pick this fellow who happened to be at the church doing some charity work. I asked him to be my stand in for my baptism. He was the witness (Godfather) for my baptism.

We had a small wedding mainly to keep her parents happy.

Moving and adding on

After living in the city for almost ten years, we decided to purchase a home in New Jersey. Her parents were not to thrill because of the inconvenient of traveling. Now the drawback was I had to pick them up when they wanted to visit.

We had our first child after being married ten years. Her mother would always complain because she could not visit when she wanted too, especially now that she had a granddaughter.

When we baptism our daughter her mother would stick her two cents in and tells us what to do and how. I ask one of my friends whom happened to be Greek to be the godfather and he was more than a happy. She even complained because he was not part of the family; it seems anything I said or suggest she would fight me.

I could not believe after being married all these years her mother would still commit on us sleeping in the same bed; This was just typical of her. I got to the point I would just let it slide off me.

Two years later we had another daughter and again continue to complain about not being able to visit as she seemed fit.

From bad to worse

As the years past her parents were still interfering with our marriage, especially her mother. She would make little remarks about our relationship. I could sense it was taking a toll on our life together. Tina seemed to be siding with parents, more and more.

Her father had gotten ill and soon after passed away. Her brother also at a young age also died.

Her mother as terrible as she was had gotten worse if that was possible and would spend more time at our house.

Tina and I started quarreling more often; it got to the point I would stay late at the office just to avoid arguing.

I was just turning the big five 0, and Tina threw me a surprise Birthday party and invited relatives and friends.

Just gets worse

Just when I thought things were getting better, she tells me the very next day she wanted a divorce. I was speechless; she starts accusing me of cheating on her and ever accused me of having an affair. I assured her none of it was true, but it went on deaf ears.

She wasted no time filing for divorce, as much as I did not want to take this route, I did not put up a fight.

I started packing my belongings and move out. I found an apartment not too far from my daughters.

When the divorce was final; I still got to see my daughter's regular.

Like mother like daughter

As the years passed, our oldest daughter had gotten married. I was not too fond of the groom, but to keep my daughter happy I just went along.

About a year later we had become grandparents, so I got to see Tina even more often. When our granddaughter was turning five years, we found out our daughter had filed for divorce. We came to know that our son-in- law was not what he seemed to be. I guess my initial feeling was correct. She received full custardy of her daughter; our granddaughter became my inspiration in life. Tina and I would continue to talk and stay in touch with each other over the years.

Never too old

The years just flew by; Tina and I stayed friends to spite the divorce and kept in touch over the years.

Fifteen years had passed, and Tina says to me, "she was on Cape Cod and fell in love with the area." She saw this house and wanted to move there and asked if I wanted to purchase it together and live there.

I was taken by surprise and said, "yes." Our daughters were ecstatic to hear the news. We moved in, and it was almost like old times, our daughters and granddaughter would visit us.

Three years later I said to Tina let's make it official and get re-married.

Today we are spending our senior years here on the Cape and travel down to Jersey to see our daughters and granddaughter.

Two guys

My name is Paula, and was born in Boston and moved to New York City when I was in my mid-teens.

Even though we had churches close to where we lived, we traveled uptown to the Greek Cathedral.

I got to meet a lot of girls my age and started to enjoy my new friends.

I also started going to some of the socials events and meet some of the guys.

I began to date this fellow who was a few years older than I. The other guys that were my age seemed to be immature. I had to make an excuse when I would see him; my sister would cover for me and warn me to be careful.

After a few dates, I realized my sister was correct, he tried to force himself on me and was not ready to get involved with him sexually.

So, I stop seeing him; the only sad part was I would see him at the socials, which made me feel uncomfortable. It got to the point I stop going.

Making new friends

I continued to stay in contact with some of the girls that I met at the Cathedral.

When I turned eighteen and graduated high school, I met this fellow named Angelo who had recently graduated from the police academy. There were two problems, he was six years older and was Italian. Something my parents would never accept. So, I had to keep it quiet. I had to sneak out and make up a story that I was going to the church club.

After seeing Angelo for a few months, I enjoyed his company and was falling for him. So, I just continued to keep it hush for now.

One of my friends invited me to go with her to the Cathedral; they had their annual dance. Angelo was not too thrilled when I told him.

At the dance, I ran into two sisters that I had made friends. We talked about thing in general, and somehow their brother comes into the conversation. He sounded like someone I would enjoy meeting. I said, "how come you never mentioned him before." The one sister says, "he was a few years older and never got involved with the church actives." I handed them my phone number and said, "maybe Michael would like to meet me for a drink."

Surprised phone call

I was just beginning to think maybe their brother was not interested. No sooner, he calls. We spoke for almost an hour; he was so easy to talk with and someone that I would like to know, and made plans to meet.

I told my parents about him, and they were happy as can be.

When I met him, his sisters were not exaggerating he was just as they describe him. In fact, even better looking. He bought candy and flowers which got my mother attention because most of the guys I dated she had her doubts.

We went to a movie and later went for a ride on the Staten Island Ferry; he was a perfect gentleman

When I got home, I told my sister I had the nicest time. She quietly says, "what about Angelo he called while you were out."

Making up my mind

I now had two fellows in my life and had affection for both. I like Angelo very much, and now Michael I took a liking to him. The hard part knowing I could not lead them both on, so had to decide. As much as I admired Michael, decided to stay with Angelo.

A few days later Michael called, I just told him the truth, and he took it like a real trooper. In a way, I was a little disappointed he did not put up any argument.

A total about face

I saw Angelo the next day, and somehow, he found out, and question me. I just told him he was a brother of some girlfriends. He got pretty upset about it and even got belligerent. I snapped back at him and said, "who do you think you are telling me you I can see." I tried to move out of the way, but he managed to smack me right in my face. I screamed and said, "don't you ever touch me again." I ran off just looking to get away.

He yells out, "you can't go too far."

For the first time in my life, I was frightened. I always heard about this happening, and now I was a victim. I got my bearings and went immediately home.

When I got to my neighborhood Angelo's car was parked down the street from my house, but no Angelo.

One of my girlfriends lived just a few blocks away so decided not to take a chance and go to her house. When I got to her apartment one of Michael's sisters was also there; when they saw my face, they asked, "what happened?"

I explained and washed up and put on a little makeup so my parents would not see my bruised face.

When I felt, it was safe Michael's sister walked me home just to be sure I was all right. His car was not there; I thank her for walking me home.

I was lucky no one was around and went straight to my room.

From two to ?

It's amazing just a short time I had two men in my life and now have none.

I told my sister, and she remarked, "What are you going to do?"

I quietly say. "please do not say one word to mom and dad."

A few days later when I got home from work, my mother tells me Michael called, and to please call him back.

I realized his sister most of said what had happened. Part of me wanted to call, but dropping him like I didn't feel right.

I was avoiding Angelo as much as possible, after what he did I was fearful.

I finally called Michael and the first thing he asked, "what happened, my sister clued me some of it; can we get together? I said, "definitely."

We met at a local bar where I had gone with Angelo. He greeted me with a hug, and without wasting a minute ask me exactly what happened. I explained the story and he comments, "not Angelo the cop."

Why?

"I know him, in fact, we hang out here."

"Oh, no I don't believe it!"

Michael says, "I never told you I was a detective, I meant to, but you dump me before getting a chance.

This guy Angelo has a short fuse, and from what I know of him he is a very jealous individual.

Michael told me to stay low key and let him try to iron this out. I was scared and had no idea what to expect. After he had smacked me, he was capable of anything.

Just gets worse.

A few days later, while coming home from work, I spotted Angelo in his patrol car waiting.

He calls to me, not to make a scene walked over to him.

The first thing he says, "so you know Mike!"

Yes, through his sister."

I have a lot of respect for Mike; he is a great guy.

Just one problem, "no one tells me what to do."

He drives off shouting, "you have not seen the last of me."

I spoke with Michael later that night and told me what he said.

He assured me not to worry.

For the next few weeks, all was fine. I had to work late this one night and was walking home; I felt that someone was following me. Was I too paranoid!

As I was walking through the doorway this shadow appears; someone tried to grab me. Angelo had taught me how to fight off an attacker and use this method to fight it off.

I was a nervous wreck and ran upstairs still shaken and called the police. I called out but, no one was home. Within minutes the police arrived.

Much to my surprise one of the officers was Angelo. I told them exactly what happened and what I did to defend myself. Angelo gave me a grin like he was sorry he taught me the art of defense.

After they filled out an incident report, Angelo says, "don't worry we will get to the bottom of this."

Later told Michael of the event. Michael asked me if I was all right. "I was so sure Angelo was behind it, but he was on duty." He said, "made sure if I had to work late take a cab."

Another time we had gone out for dinner this individual comes up to our table and starts talking to me and getting very belligerent. Michael nicely asked him to leave, and he told Michael to mind his own business. Michael stands up and again says, "leave." He tries to take a swing at Michael, but Michael with a hit to his face takes the guy down.

Michael called management to have them call the police. Within minutes they arrive, call it a coincidental Angelo shows up. Michael spoke with Angelo and then took the guy into custardy.

I started getting nasty phone calls at work. The phone calls continued to get worse, and I could not do my job. As frequent as I was getting those nasty phone calls, they stopped. Michael told me he took care of the problem

Problem solved

He said he realized it was too much of a coincidence that Angelo seemed always to show up. So, he decided to do a little detective investigation.

The guy that came to the restaurant seemed to be orchestrated by Angelo, in fact, he was also the same guy who tried to scare you that night. He confessed to all of it.

Angelo got suspended until his hearing. Michael said you might be asked to testify.

When the news hit the newspaper, other girls came out of the closet. My testimony was not necessary because they had enough evidence. The trial seemed to drag out. Angelo was found guilty and sentenced to twenty-five to thirty years.

Just the two of us

Once this was all behind us; we were seeing each other every weekend and sometimes during the week.

We went to Atlantic City to celebrate my birthday and had dinner at this fancy restaurant. When the waiter served us the appetizer, I see this shining item in with the shrimp. I pick up this beautiful diamond ring and just stare at it for a moment.

He gets up and walks over to me and gets on one knee. He takes the ring and says, "will you marry me!" With so much joy I screamed out "yes," while he is putting it on my finger. The other customers started applauding, "I was too excited to be embarrassed."

After dinner, we drove home to show my family and his and give them the good news.

We got married just about a year later and blessed with four daughters and six grandchildren.

Unfortunately, Michael was killed in the line of duty by an unknown assailant just before he was due to retire.

How the West conquered love

This story was told to me by my 80-year-old grandfather and goes back four generations. His grandfather was just seventeen when his parents decided to go west.

It was 1876 when they packed up all the belonging and went west looking for a new life. His grandfather was named Frank and was the oldest of four children.

It took them most of six months before there reached their destination, but before they arrived, they went thru hell.

Besides the inclement weather, they had to fight off bandits as well as Indians.

There were days they saw nothing but trees and blue skies and abandoned wagons, not to mentioned grave sites.

They were a month on the trail when they came across bandits that stole some of their belongings. There was no law and order; it was fighting back or giving in. Franks father was a simple man and would not put up a fight knowing he might be jeopardizing his life or even his family. By the time the rest of the train wagon realized what had happened the bandits were far gone.

Frank could not accept this and decided to act if it happened again. He had got friendly with one of the drivers who had his share of bandits before retiring as a US Marshall. So, without wasting any time, Frank asks him to show him how to use a six-shooter.

Sharpshooter

When they stop for the day, he started teaching Frank the proper way of using a six shooter. So, he would practice every chance he got.

This one day this young girl heard the shooting and decided to investigate. Not realizing she startle Frank and shouts out, "Are you trying to get yourself shot." She apologized and says, "we have been hearing gun shots every day about the same time and were curious what all that shooting was about." Frank explained, and she said, "you feel that's the only way to prevent this."

"Yes," Frank shouts out.

She says her name is, "Annie."

Annie says, "may I see your gun."

She takes aim and shoots a small branch that was about 25 yards away. Frank was amazed, "where did you learn to shoot?"

"I have been shooting since I was ten years' old, and won many ribbons."

He continued his practicing and Annie would give a few tips; within a short time became Frank so fast and accurate it was incredible.

Annie took a liken to Frank.

Times change

This one day, everything seemed quiet maybe too quiet. Suddenly all they heard was screaming from afar. It was an Indian attack, the leader shouts, "make a circle and take cover." The wagons go into position, and everyone is taking cover for their lives. Franks family is taking cover when suddenly an arrow with a flame hits their wagon, and in a matter of seconds, starts burning.

They all leap out of the flaming wagon and take cover at one of the other wagons. Some of the other travels help Frank, and his father put out the flames before it was a total loss.

As there putting out the fire, an Indian leap's knocking Frank unconscious. Just before the Indian is ready to use his knife on Frank, a gunshot rings out, and the Indian falls dead.

Minutes later the Indians retreat, and Frank starts regaining consciousness. The first thing he saw was Annie leaning over him tending his wound with a wet cloth and saying, "what happened."

Frank's father shouts out, "Annie saved your life."

He slowly gets up and gives Annie a hug, and says, "I own you my life."

The leader of the wagon train says, "be ready for another attack with even more force."

Sure, enough within minutes they started attacking. Annie and Frank stood side by side shooting at the Indians. Between both, they killed more than a third of the enemy. Annie sees the Chief takes careful aim and fires. The chief falls dead, and the Indians entirely stop fighting and retreat.

The wagon leader shouts out, "let's get moving because once they pick a new chef they will return and we may not be as lucky."

They continued and when they felt it was safe, stopped for the night.

Disaster

The day started out sunny and hot, but within hours the sky turned gray and scary. The winds began to whip up leaving visibility unbearable. From afar they could see a funnel cloud touch down picking up anything in its path tearing trees from their roots and heading in their direction. All they could do was take cover where ever possible and pray.

Within minutes the funnel cloud came crashing thru the wagon train with a deafening sound of death. When the smoke cleared, dozen laid dead and many injured. Frank went looking for Annie's wagon, but all he found was debris where their wagon once was. He searches the area and saw other wagon torn apart like paper, and bodies tossed around like dolls. One of the men who were also searching the area shouts out to Frank, "come quickly." When he got to where Annie's wagon landed, all they saw was her family bodies intact, but no Annie. Another survivor shouts, "come quickly."

Frank sees Annie lying still. He picks up her head and is trying to revive her; suddenly she starts moaning.

Annie screams out, "my family are they okay?"

All she remembered was jumping out of the wagon to release the horses, and the wagon just tore apart and went airborne.

Frank took her into his arms and sadly said, "they did not make it." Annie starts crying, Frank holding her in his arms says, "they are in Haven."

Moving forward

They buried the bodies and tendered the injured.

Annie salvaged some of her belongings she could find and continued the trip with Franks family.

The days turned into weeks, and it was rough going, but they managed to overcome any small problems.

When they hit the mountains, they ran into heavy snow and frigid temperatures. Now it was a matter of fighting mother nature.

Franks younger sister had developed pneumonia and just got worse. It got to the point she was on the edge of dying. Nothing seemed to work. When everything else failed, Annie decided to try some old fashion remedies that her mother had used. It was like a miracle; within days she was up and alert. Frank realized she was like a God sent, first him now his sister.

The snow was deep and slowing the wagons down pushing they off schedule, but as the trail boss said, "better late than never."

Final after weeks of traveling thru the snow they saw green pastures from afar, realizing their journey was almost over.

When they arrived, Frank had a different outlook on Annie, love just conquer Franks', heart.

He asks Annie to marry him; she happily replied, "yes."

Finally, after months of traveling, they reached their destination. Once they settled in, they were married a short time later.

Annie became a showgirl, and they travel the country doing what they did well together.

Years later they settled in Oklahoma.

They only had one son, and many nieces and nephews and devoted much of their love to them, and the rest is History.

Neighborhood sweethearts

My name is Hercules, yes, I got teased when I was younger. But when I got into high school that changed, being a 6'2 freshman, I got respect.

We were a family of seven and were a very close family. The only downsize our parents were old fashion, especially our mother.

Our father had gotten ill and passed away, leaving mom with a financial hardship.

Our older brother was working part time while in was in High school. I felt the need also to help, so I also got a part-time job after school. So, I found a job after school doing delivers for the neighborhood grocery store. We both gave mom our money to help with the bills and food shopping.

Cover up

I met this girl named Lorraine while making deliver's and we became friends.

I would sneak around my mother, but somehow, she found out and would question me.

I would, of course, deny it.

So, I would play it cool.

The only one who knew was my older brother.

I would tell my mother I was getting involved with after-school projects; this was the only way I could get to see Lorraine after school without drawing any suspicion.

I felt that I was not earning enough so came my junior year decided to quit school and got a full-time job. Mom was not thrilled with the idea. I told my mother not to worry; I will go to night school to earn my diploma.

So, I started working full time at a local butcher shop in the neighborhood. Lorraine would come in and do some shopping, and we talk. Just my luck my mother also comes in to do her shopping and see us talking.

Again, I would deny any association except her shopping.

So, I had to be extra careful and came to find out there were a lot of nosy neighbors.

Taking a chance

When I turned eighteen, I got my license and wanted a car badly. The problem was I could not afford the insurance. The law then was anyone twenty-five, and older did not require auto insurance. So being shrewd I put the car in my mother's name, knowing she would never sign for me. I signed her name.

Not to draw attention, I would garage the car at my boss's house.

Everything was going fine; this one night I decided to skip night school and go for a joy ride with Lorraine. Because it was the school night, I had to be home my usual time to avoid questing.

We drove around for a little while and stopped to get a snack. I was pulling out of a parking spot and hit the car in front. Knowing I had no insurance and the car was under my mother's name I panic and drove off.

I returned the car to my boss's house and took Lorraine home. I went back as like nothing happened.

When I got home, there were two men in suits talking to my mother. "Where have you been," as my mom is shouting and trying to hit me with the broom. The two men had to hold her back from hitting me. She goes on yelling, "what is going on they are telling me that my car was in an accident, what car!"

It seems when I hit the other car my bumper came off with the license plate attached. With my mother's limited English, I could get around and explain to the detective's what happened. Making it sound like the car was properly registered, and everything documented.

We worked it out and had to pay the damages and a small fine.

My mother gave me a lecture that I would never forget.

Saying things like, "I know you're seeing that girl."

"I bet you were with that night!

I never tried to second guess mom; "she had a six sense."

Short break up

To keep my mother happy, I stop seeing Lorraine and would date some Greek girls to keep mom pleased. I just kept a low profile and would not say anything, realizing we would just argue.

After dating other girls, I came to realize that I had much more than affection for Lorraine and started seeing her again.

I did not want my mother getting upset, so I tried to make her understand. I guess telling my mom was not the right thing to do, all we did was argue.

When I turned, twenty decided to join the army reserve, before getting drafted. I felt maybe being away for a short time my mother would mellow out; was it wish full thinking!

I got stationed at Ft. Bliss Oklahoma; I would call and write hoping to get mom soften up; they say times heals almost everything. I told Lorraine when I come back permanently we would tell my mother our intentions and was hoping mom would have a chance to mellow.

Shocking changes

Now that I was home it was time to give mom the news about our plans. I wanted to catch her in a good mood. So, I decided to tell her Sunday after church while having lunch.

Even before I could tell her everything in detail, she starts yelling, saying things like, "with all the girls within your heritage you are getting involved with an outsider!" She went on and on with no sign of letting up. My older brother came to my rescue, and try to make her understand we are living in a new era.

When she quieted down, I told mom that Lorraine was going to convert to our faith. Mom says, "what." It seemed to help because her attitude took a total change.

Mom said, "when did this come about; when do I get to meet her?"

I was happy hearing her say that.

So, I invited Lorraine to a Sunday dinner; this was going to be the big test. Lorraine came with a bunch of flowers and was nervous.

We all sat down to eat, and mom in her broken English started asking Lorraine different questions. She kept her cool and believed me when I say that was tough.

Mom was impressed with her sweet personality; when she left gave Lorraine a hug. We both felt a side of relief.

Lorraine wasted no time and started going for classes at our church. My mother was happy that she took this avenue.

Planning for the big day

While Lorraine was going weekly for her transformation to our religion, we also started to make plans for our wedding.

My mother began to put her ideas into our plans and Lorraine was not too thrilled. They would have slight disagreements, and of course, I was in the middle of it all. We all lived within a few blocks of each other and wanted our mothers to meet. Lorraine's mom invited my mom for coffee, and I could sense she was not so eager to go but eventually, went. It felt good that they got together even if it was only for a short time.

They discussed the wedding and said what they had to say which just made things even more problematic.

We just yes, and did what we felt would be more realistic.

As the time got, nearer things had gotten to the point they would invite whoever they both felt was "Politically Correct." In their eyes, you cannot invite one without inviting the other

We had nearly two hundred people of which one-quarter they invited.

I guess just seeing they both happy, and content was worth it.

All went well, which was a blessing!

We spent our honeymoon in the Caribbean Islands.

A short time later we purchased a home in Long Island.

We had three children and six grandchildren.

Not my choice

My name is Angie and was born in Athens Greece and came to America in the early 50's. We were a family of five, and I was the youngest.

We all attend church every Sunday rain or snow. My parents were very religious and followed our faith to the tee.

My brothers were at the age where they would be dating. They knew they better be Greek, or all hell would break out.

So, they dated Greek girls to keep our parents content. They would tease me saying, "you better only date Greek boys."

Our church had a social club and got to meet a lot of Greek boys my age. So, because of that, it kept my parents happy.

First date

When I turned eighteen, my parents allowed me to date. But my father had to meet the boy first, no exceptions.

I met this fellow Michael; he was a few months younger than me; In fact, our parents knew each other. We both graduated the same year just different schools. We went together to both our proms and would see each other every weekend.

Came September we both left for college he went out of state, and I went to a local university. My father did like the idea of me going off to an out of state school.

I also wanted to get a part-time job, but my dad banned it and, he wanted me to concentrate on my school work.

Michael and I kept in touch and would get together when we were between semesters and holidays.

Time changes everything

After we both graduate Michael left for the Navy to proceed his new career. I was going to enjoy the summer before starting my new career in the world of business.

When my father heard this, he began to change his tune. He would get involved with my social life. It seems he met a Greek fellow who just came to America on a visa and wanted me to help him get acquainted with the American way. That how he put it. I felt strange, but my mother assured me it was nothing but a friendly jester. When I met, him I had to admit he was good looking, and a lot older than I came to believe. My father slipped me some money and asked me to show him the sights. I spoke Greek fluently so I could communicate with him. We spent the day sightseeing and had dinner later that night.

My father wanted me to continue to entertain him. Now I was sorry I did not start working sooner; so, I saw him for the next few weeks.

My father even invited him for Sunday dinner.

I asked my brothers for their advice. They said, "just keep dad happy."

Then it happens my father told me to do another favor. I said, "like what?" "I want you to marry him so that he could stay in America."

"Then after it all legal, you will get a divorce or get it annulled."

"No, no I promised you I would show him around and nothing else!" We argue something I never did before with my dad.

I was in tears and ran into my room.

I loved my father and would do most anything for him, but I just felt he went too far.

I wanted so badly to talk to Michael, but he was still on active duty with no way of getting ahold of him, until he contacts me.

Time heals most

A few days later my father says to me have you thought it out. I said, "Father I love you, please do not put me into this kind of situation." My father says, "well keep thinking about it."

I landed a job with a large business firm in Wall Street and was scheduled to start in under two weeks.

I spoke with Michaels parents, and they told me he would be finishing his training and getting a commission. They invited me to join them for his military exercises.

I told my parents I was going away next week to attend Michael's military graduation.

My father was upset because it seemed he had other plans; I made it clear that I had no intentions to get involved with his friend's marriage plans.

After Michaels graduation, he took a fourteen-day leave before departing for a nine-month deployment at sea.

They say time does wonder because my feeling for Michael had reached a new height. My love had gotten stronger, and he felt the same.

I told Michael what my father wanted me to do. You did the right thing by making him realize your feelings; we spoke about our future.

When Michael left, my father started up again. I made it clear that I love Michael and that was the end of the conversation.

End of the roar

My father went on deaf ears because he kept bringing it up. So, I told my parents that I was moving. I made up a story because I did not want my mother getting upset if I told how the real reason. My father did not like the idea living on my own. He would lecture me on going out into the world on my own.

I kept it quiet when I started looking for an apartment. I wanted it close to my job; the trouble was the rents were a little more than my budget. I kept looking, but it was the same problem.

One of the girls from the office says, "how would you like a roommate; I have the same problem." Knowing this was the only way, I was excited when she asks.

When I told my parents, all hell broke out, between my mother and especially my father. I made it clear that I was moving and that was final. Every day my dad would argue and just go on and on. My mother came around and understood; she even helped with some of the furnishes.

The transformation

Michael was scheduled to be home within the month and was looking forward to seeing him. My father seemed to have mellow out; he would occasionally say something, and I just yes him.

When Michael got home, we got together, and he told me about his new assignment. He said he received a desk job for the Navy in Washington DC.

He wanted me to go live with him. I said I loved the idea, but my parents would never agree and living together, forget that. Michael says, "Okay let's get married."

I was happy to hear him say that. I told Michael fine, but I want to get engaged, then we could plan for our marriage."

We went that same week and looked at rings, and told our parents.

Both our parents threw us an engagement party.

We would see each other almost every weekend, either he came here, or I see him. My father would make his general remarks when I went to see him, but mom would just tell me to loosen up.

We were married a year later and lived just outside DC in Virginia, and have three beautiful daughters.

Double cross

It all started when I was just turning the ripe age of 20. My name is Mark; I lived with my older brother and younger sister and of course my parents.

Working as a bank teller was not what I wanted to do as a career, but it had its rewards. I got to meet a lot of girls.

My father was easy going, but my mother was a tough one. She felt we should all marry within our faith.

So, to keep my mother happy I dated girls that were our faith. My mom would always make a remark whenever I dated a different girl. I would just say, "I am looking for Mrs. right."

Keeping mother happy

One day while coming back from lunch I see this most beautiful girl; it was love at first sight. I managed to get her attention, and we started talking and came to realize she was of my faith. I ask to see her again; I had to pinch myself, she was beautiful and my faith.

That night, told my mother that I met the girl I want to marry. My mom was beholding and says, "you just met her, and besides you date so many what makes you think she is the one?"

"Wait till you meet her, and you will see."

The more we dated, the more I was sure she was the girl for me.

Mom later said, "invite her over for a Sunday dinner." Everyone loved her; she had beauty, personality and not to mention very sexily, and our faith.

We dated for well over a year, and we were getting serious.

Change of plans

I was checking the mail and notice a letter from Uncle Sam. It did not take a genius to know what it was. Just holding the envelope gave me the empty feeling. I had thirty days before reporting.

When I told my family, there were mixed emotions. Mary was not very happy when I told her. We spent almost every day together, talking about our future.

The Vietnam war had just broken out, and that's all we read in the newspaper and heard on the radio and television.

My family gave me a going away party, and I took it one step further I asked Mary to marry me. So, we got engaged, and we made it official. We would get married when I returned from active duty.

The night before leaving I assured her nothing was going to get in the way of our relationship. I never felt this depressed before; I was not alone with my feelings. I made many friends who felt the same way. I became very close to one of them during our basic and advanced training.

After the first half of our training, Mary came to see me. I introduce Mary to my new friend Ronald, and some of the other guys.

Bad news

After we had completed our advanced training, we got our assignments. Most of us were going to Vietnam, something I was afraid would happen. My friend Ronald was staying stateside for now.

When I told Mary, she broke down and started crying, thinking the worse. I told her to think positive.

They gave us two weeks to get ready for our new assignment. So, we spent every day together.

When we arrived in Vietnam, you could hear the war in the far horizon. We said our goodbyes and good luck to each other. They broke us up into different groups, not knowing anything until we were assigned.

I went to this compound with two other soldiers; the others were picked up by a large transport truck. There was no doubt they were heading into harm's way.

A slight turn around

The good news was I going to work as envoy'. My assignment was to work with the locals and our troops for enhancing support. But my job did not end there. Every day soldiers were being killed or severely wounded. I had to identify and have their remains sent back to the states this was a depressing job. I just learned to accept it or land up in a straitjacket.

Once I got settled in wrote my family and Mary to give them some good news, if that was possible. I also wrote Ronald to give him some update.

The only sound thing was getting mail from Mary and my family.

I'll never forget the day when headquarters had gotten attacked by the enemy; it was the one time I had to use my weapon to defend myself. Thanks to our Marines they came to fight off the enemy who were the Viet Cong.

After being here well over six months, I learned a lot. In my eyes, this war was not being fought to win; which made me more resentful.

Disappointment

Mary would write me three to four times a week. Her words were not the same, and shortly after no mail. I wrote her serval times, but she never responded. I even wrote my family hoping to get some light on what was going on.

My sister sent me a letter; she hardly wrote me, so I knew something was not right. When I read the letter, I was in disbelief and speechless. Somehow Mary got the impression I was seeing a native girl and was very involved. I wrote her again trying to explain it was not true, and where she got this crazy rumor.

I still had three months on my tour. Knowing there was no way to get to the bottom of this scandal, I had no choice but wait till I got back home.

After two weeks, she never answered me, and I became very hostile. My sergeant even noticed my behavior and questioned me. I showed him the letter, and he even gave a chuckle.

He says, "When did you find the time to have an affair?" He suggested he would write her a letter and explain, "it's not true."

I said, "she will think I put you up to it."

"I'm afraid nothing can work till I get home."

About a month before being scheduled to leave I received a letter from Mary. To my surprise, it was a Dear John. I was in total denial.

I just thought it out and realized the only one person who could be behind this had to be my good friend, Ronald.

The truth will prevail

I told nobody the exact date I was coming home. I had to convince Mary that everything she heard was not true. I knew just telling her was not going to win her back; otherwise, she would have done so in the letters.

When I got home, my family was happy to see me. My mother says, "Why did you do something that stupid and get involved with a Vietnam girl." I assured her it was not true, and where did you hear that story.

She said, "Mary told us."

I said, "well it's not true."

My mother said, "deep down I did believe it."

I said, "I will get to the bottom of this!" I had to get some answer, after three months of waiting I could wait no longer.

The next morning, I went to where Mary worked and patiently waited. I saw her coming, and she looked just as beautiful as I remember her.

When she saw me, it was like she saw a ghost.

"What are you doing here," she mutters?

"I must talk to you and get this rumor past us."

She says, "I cannot talk now."

I said, "What time do you finish work?"

She fires back, "I have nothing to say."

"Yes, but I do, and I love you with all my heart."

I could sense she was not herself.

She says, "Okay, I'll see you right here at five."

When I saw her again, I just melted and tried to give her a kiss, but she turned her face. We went to a local restaurant to try and iron this out.

I say, "do you not love me anymore?

"I don't know, what you did I could never forgive you."

"But that's the problem I did nothing to hurt you."

"Where did you ever get that impression, because it's just an ugly rumor."

She hesitated, then says, "your friend Rod told me."

The drink I had in my hand I crushed the glass when she said that.

She says, "you're bleeding" and reaches for a napkin and puts it on my wound.

My feeling was right on Ronald was behind this.

"Why would he say that if it were not true."

"I wish I knew; I thought he was a friend."

She takes my hand and kisses it and says, "I'm such a fool."

"What about Rod, he said he was going to see me tonight."

"Leave it to me I'll straighten him out!"

"Please don't do anything crazy."

Gratification

I took her home and waited patiently for my so-called friend.

It was over thirteen months since we saw each other.

This sports car pulls up and parks, and sure enough, my dear friend is getting out. He hadn't changed since seeing him last; he walks into view and stops dead in his track.

I could sense his edginess when he realized it was me, as he says, "what are you doing here?"

I reply, "no what are you doing here!"

He was speechless, but not me.

I blasted him like there was no tomorrow.

"You call yourself a friend, starting dirty rumors taking advantage of me and especially Mary."

"Did you think you could get away with this?"

I realize friends like this; one needs no enemies.

I told him, "leave and don't look back."

Later, I came to find out he took a gamble, which I would never come home.

Reuniting

I called Mary after my encounter with my ex-friend.

She apologized, for being so open minded. I told her, "it's water under the bridge."

The next day I put the ring back on her finger.

I told my family the good news, and when my active duty is complete, we will start arrangements for the wedding.

I did my remaining duty only two hours away. So, I would come home every weekend.

We were married about eighteen months later and had the most beautiful wedding.

Today we have five beautiful children and six grandchildren.

I could dance all night

My name is Ralf and lived in Manhattan with my parents and two younger sisters.

I loved music and dancing; I go to many of the local dance halls just to watch others dance when I was not dancing.

My mother would say, "is anything else you can do but dance."

I try to explain that I enjoyed it and wanted to become a ballroom dancer.

I dance with many girls, but the ones I met were more interested in other things like getting married.

When I turned twenty-one, I started going to a dance hall called Roseland and met a lot of couples who were dance lovers.

Meeting the right partner

I go every Saturday night to Roseland and dance, this one night I saw this couple dancing, and the girl caught my attention. Call it intuition, but something about her just got to me. She had a stunning body, but that was not the reason. She danced as she was floating on air, and her movements were like I have never seen before.

When I saw her at the bar by herself, approach her and said, "May I buy you a drink. I introduce myself, and tells me her name is, "Irene." We spoke for a few minutes, then ask her to dance. Irene was light on her feet it felt like we were dancing on air; we dance a few more dances, and she says, "I have to go." Before

I could say anything, she walked off thanking me for the dances. Deep down I knew she was the kind of dance partner I needed.

For the next few Saturdays, I saw her dancing with the same fellow realizing there must be something between them.

I went to the bar to have a drink and started making chit chat with the bartender. He says to me, "you look like you lost your best friend." I asked him about Irene, and he says, "do mean Irene and Jack." I pointed them out, "yes, those two." The bartender says, "they been coming here forever, and the funny part is they are brother and sister." My mouth must have fallen to the floor, "you got to be joking," I happily say.

Making my move

Not wasting a minute, I immediately went over to her while she was sitting and said, "Hello." She introduced me, and never mention it was her brother. I just went along and asked, "Do you mind if I dance with Irene."

He says, "fine."

After a few dancers, she tells me that "Jack is her brother." When I first saw, you dancing you caught my attention. She says, "that's the reason." "No, no that is not why."

"Yes, you do have a beautiful figure; It was the way you dance, that caught my attention."

She asks me, "how long have you been dancing?" I reply, "just about a year."

She tells her brother, "if you want to leave, Ralf will see me home."

I tell her, "I want to dance, professionally." Irene tells me, it's going to take a lot of practice and time. I took her home, and Irene said, "if you're willing to try I'll see you next Saturday."

My first professional dance lesson

I could not wait till Saturday and felt like a kid. Even my mother would commit on my behavior.

I got there early, much to my surprise she was already there with her brother and walked over to where they were dancing.

Her brother says, "have fun."

She takes my hand, and we went to a back room, I never knew even existed. She showed me some new moves, and we practice for well over an hour.

She had me practice on my own just to get the feeling. Then we dance the night away.

By the end of the evening, I was a score. Even my feet were tired. I used mussels that I did not know existed.

We sat down, and Irene says, "how do you feel."

I had to admit I was tired.

She takes off my shoes and rubs my feet.

"Do you still want to continue?"

"More than ever."

I took her home and made plans to get together and practice during the week.

Getting more involved

We continued dancing during the week and of course Roseland on Saturday night.

It was incredible how my dancing went from what I thought was decent to all most professional.

Many of the couples compliment us on our dancing, including her brother.

Irene got tickets to go to what was called the Harvest Moonball dancing contest at Madison Garden. After the performance, we stopped for a few drinks.

I said, "we should apply next year ourselves."

She says, "are you serious."

"Yes, with all my heart."

"I always dream about it," Irene's says.

"I never found a partner whoever wanted too, not even my brother."

"It's going to take a lot more practice, and commit."

Between work and practicing, I realized this was going to take 100% commit if we were going to succeed.

Irene was a real trooper she stayed on top of everything.

If she thought I was slacking off, she told me.

Getting serious

We were just weeks away from the big day, and I was nervous. Not Irene, I never knew a girl that was so positive and so focus. She gave me the confidence I needed.

We decided to dance the Viennese waltz for our competition.

I told her, "win or lose let's take a vacation."

Irene said, "I love the idea, where would you want to go?"

"How about a cruise, to the Caribbean islands?"

She gave me a hug, and I just kissed her right smack on her lips. At first, she backs off and then kissed me back. I said, "you realize we have been together all these months and all we did was dance."

Irene was a couple of years older, and she would bring it up at times. But I could care less; I knew now she was more than a dance partner.

We continue to practice up until the big day. We did a dress practice; she wore this beautiful long dress, and I wore a tux with tails to get the feel.

It was a good thing she suggests the idea because I never realize the difference with the dance moves.

Irene had me so confident I felt like we were winners even before the competition started.

I'll never forget that night when the judges announced our names as the first-place winners; I had tears in my eyes. Both our dream had come to surpass.

We took that cruise we were talking about, and we welcome the change of surroundings.

While we were on our cruise, they announced our names while we were dancing. So, we gave a small sample of our dance performances, and we danced the night away.

Permanent Partners

When we returned from our getaway cruise, I was going to ask Irene to marry me. I spoke with her brother and told him my attention, and he was more than happy to hear that.

Her Birthday was coming up and felt this would be a good time to ask her.

I wanted this to be a special night, so we went to a restaurant named Longchamp's where they had a live band and dancing.

After we had dinner and before we had dessert handed her birthday gift.

She opened it up and says, "I love musical jewelry boxes."

I said, "now open it."

I'll never forget the look on her face when she opened it.

She was speechless, I got up and ask her to marry me.

She also gets up and hugs me with a kiss and says, "yes, yes."

After we finish dinner, we went to tell our family the news.

For all the time, we saw each other this was the first time I would meet her parents; they knew of me from dancing.

They congratulation us and her father asked me a lot of questions.

The next day I took her to meet my family and were they surprised because not once did I ever mention marriage.

We did not want a big wedding, but her parents, as well as mine, did not agree with us. We kept trying to convince them, but they still insisted.

It was a no-win situation.

So, after many disputes with our families, we decided to elope.

We knew there would be a lot of disagreements and disappointments. We both loved our parents and agreed it was our life and no one was going to make our plans.

Without thinking twice and telling not a soul, we flew to Las Vegas. We tied the knot, spent the weekend and flew back to tell our families.

Both our families were very disappointed, but over time they mellow out.

We continued going to Roseland almost every Saturday for the years to come.

We were upset when Roseland shut their doors after all that's where it all began.

Last Dance

After we both had retired, we did a lot of traveling, taking vacations, cruises, and seeing the world and dance the night's away.

We had just returned from taking a vacation in the far east, and my partner had taken ill.

Irene was in and out of the hospital. Then this one time she never came home. After almost forty years I had lost my partner.

We never had children, only because we felt we could not give the time, love and the attention they desired.

Now that I'm by myself, I realize the loneliness in my heart by not having a family of our own.

Jealous or love

I t is amazing how life can be effective by others. My name is Maria, and it was just my younger sister Cynthia and our parents.

Our parents came to America in the early 40's. It was rough at the beginning my father had to stretch every penny he earned to put food on our table and clothing on our backs.

When I was in my teens, my sister always tried to steal the attention; If I received any reward at school for anything, she would try to make herself look better. If I didn't feel well, my sister would complain that she felt sick. My mother would give her the attention. I just learned to ignore it.

Being a good sister

I was permitted to go on a date when I turned eighteen. My first date was a boy from the neighborhood, and of course, my parents had to approve.

Just to start trouble, my sister would tell our parents lies about my dates. So, it made things more difficult to enjoy myself.

I started attending a church social group where I met boys and girls my age. When my sister turned eighteen, our parents asked me to take her to the club. So being a good Samaritan, I took her to the next gathering. For the first few times, everything was fine.

Spoke too soon

One of the girls from our group invited a fellow she met at another church social club. She introduces me to him; his name was Mitch and had just gotten discharged from the Navy. While Mitch and I were making conversation, my sister walks over to us and makes a sarcastic remark. I immediately apologized, "don't mind her she is my younger sister." He comments, "I have one just like her too!"

We chatted most of the night and my sister continued to be a pest and kept coming over and being annoying and kept saying, "I want to go home."

I gave Mitch my phone number and went home.

No sooner we get back she tells our parents that I met a guy.

A few days later Mitch calls, and we made plans to see each other.

He picks me up and meets my parents, and of course, my sister is making her usual sarcastic remarks.

After we dated a few times, he asks me to go steady.

I like Mitch and agreed.

Not even a month goes by, and my sister tells me she is seeing a guy she met at the church club. I say, "I did not even know you were seeing anyone: do mom and dad know?"

"No, don't you say anything."

"Why you seem always to tell them when I meet someone."

She goes on with her usually sarcastic ways, "I will tell them when I'm ready."

Being vindictive

After seeing Mitch for about six months, my father says, "what are your intentions with this fellow?"

I tried to explain that I'm only seeing him a short time; why do you ask?"

"You are not getting any younger."

I told Mitch what my father said; Mitch spoke with my dad in private and said he got things ironed out for now. He never said the exact extent of the conversation, and I never question him.

While having super, my sister says, "I have news I want to tell you all, I'm getting engaged." Our parents were shocked to hear this as well as I.

Our father says, "who is this person and why did we not even know."

"He is from the church club, and is a very nice guy."

"You will meet him shortly."

She told me whom he was and seemed nice from what I saw of him. He was a few years older than my sister, in fact even me.

He had to be some special kind of person to take her sarcastic remarks and knowing my sister he was in for a rude awaking.

Our parents took a likely to him; my father looks at me and says, "it should be you who is getting engaged."

I said, "in due time!"

Deep down I felt she was spiteful, again this was typical of her.

When I told Mitch, even he was shocked and said, "I did not even know she was seeing anyone."

"That makes two of us; I was just as surprised."

Mitch ask me, "Do you know this fellow?"

"Yes, but only seeing him and saying hello a few times at the church socials."

Things turn around

A short time later Mitch pops the question, and we got engaged. My dad was as happy as could be and says, "we will have a twin engagement party." I could sense my sister was not thrilled because she wanted all the attention.

A week before the party our father had a heart attack and passed away.

Now instead of having a happy celebration, we were in mourning. At the wake, I got to meet and make conversation with my sister's boyfriend Charles. He was low key and get along type of guy. I realize now this was how he could tolerate my sister's attitude. Even Mitch agreed and says, "he is too good for her."

Charles told me in confidence, "your sister was the one that wanted to rush into getting engaged." He goes on and says, "I wanted to wait and save some money and get established, before this all came about." "In fact, I still do more than ever, now that your father passed away."

"Yes, out of respect Mitch and I are going to wait about a year." Charlie agreed, "that's smart, I'll try to convince your sister."

Knowing my sister, I tell him, "good luck."

Mitch and I were planning a small wedding, and have the reception at the church hall. My sister remarks, "we are going to have a large wedding and have the reception at the Statler Hotel."

My sister problem was, she had champagne taste, but beer pocket money.

We both felt sorry for Charles, thank God, he had the common sense.

Preparing for the big day

We had planned our wedding day and booked the church hall.

My sister also planned her wedding day and waited till after ours. When I question her, she just remarks we like the late fall.

I went shopping for my wedding gown. After purchasing mine, my sister went shopping for hers; she comments mine cost a lot more than yours.

We had three bride maids; she had four.

Again, this was just typical of her.

Mitch suggested that from now on do not mention anything to your sister on our wedding plans.

After a few weeks, it was getting to her.

She would ask me where are you going for your honeymoon.

I would say I don't know, "Mitch wants to surprise me."

She got to the point it was almost impossible to live with her.

Mitch had wanted to purchase a home on Long Island. I loved the idea and would never even discuss it when my sister was around.

Somehow, she found out and mentioned it to me, and would just deny it.

When I told Mitch, he remarks, "I can believe her, if anything we have to live far from her maybe move out of state."

On our own

Our wedding was a picture-perfect day, and everything went well. We spent our honeymoon taking a cruise around the Greek islands.

My sister's wedding was not as picture perfect. We had an unusually early snowstorm, and leave it at that.

We purchased a home in Connecticut, far enough yet close enough to visit our parents.

We have three beautiful daughters and six grandchildren.

As for my sister, I reserve no comments!

Young and foolish

My name is Stacy and was one of five children. Our parents were from Europe and were old fashion.

I was the oldest of my sisters, and younger than my brothers. I was always helping my mother with most of the house chores. So, between school and homework and helping my mom, I kept busy.

When I turned sixteen, my family gave me a birthday party, and I invited all my friends. I met this fellow that my brother invited and took a liking to him. Call it a teenage crush and would do anything to see him again. The trouble was he was four years older.

When I asked my father, he said a blunt "no!"

I had no choice but to go behind his back.

My brother whom invited Chris said, "you're taking a big chance by going against father wishes."

Taking a chance

I had to admit I was a nervous the first time I snuck out to meet Chris.

I did not even tell my brother I was seeing him, mainly because he even warned me not to go behind dad's back.

The only time I saw him was after school, so I had to keep it hush and meet him away from the school grounds.

Somehow my mother found out I was seeing Chris and question me. I at first denied it but realized I better come clean with her. "Why are you going against your father wishes did he not say, no?"

I told my mother, "I like him."

"You are young, and have your whole life ahead of you."

"If your father finds out, there will be hell to pay!"

I continued to see him after school.

After seeing Chris for over six months on a regular basis, he suddenly stopped showing up.

I had no way of getting ahold of him and had no one to turn too. I even question my brother.

My life changes

After a month, I good no longer take the suspense of why Chris just disappeared out of my life. It wasn't like we had a fight or argument, then I could maybe understand. I question my brother again about Chris; he said, he met him at his job and was not sure about his last name or where he lived. In fact, "I haven't seen him for a while."

I went to the local police station to report him missing. The police sergeant laughs and says, "we cannot file a missing report on someone because he stops seeing you; besides you don't even know where he lives and not sure of his last name."

A few weeks later I get a phone call, from the sergeant to come and see him. Without wasting a second run down to see what had expired. The sergeant says, "it's a long shot, and maybe he could be your lost friend, he appears to have the same physical description you had told me." He goes on and says, "it is not a pleasant site he was fish out of Hudson River just a few days, ago."

"When can I see him?"

"We have a picture of his remains."

When I saw the picture, it looked nothing like him, and I could not make an identification.

A few hours later his family identifies his remains, and it turned out to be Chris.

The final report was that it was suicide.

I only knew Chris for a short time and found it hard to accept the findings.

So, I question the sergeant about the report.

He says, "why would you think otherwise?"

"Chris was not suicidal."

He promised me he would do some more investigation, and said, "Do not expect any changes."

Life goes on

Even though I was only sixteen, I could pass for older and took advantage of it and would start going to the night spots with my girlfriends.

I would meet a lot of guys, but no one could fill Chris shoes.

When I turned eighteen and graduated high school, I got a full-time job working as a file clerk.

I got to meet a lot of new friends and became close with a few of the girls.

One of them lived in Brooklyn and invited me to a night spot she hung out.

While we were having a drink, I spot this guy who resembled Chris, same smile and a lot of his features. Not to look like I was being forward, approached him and said, "Hello." He looked at me with his beautiful dark eyes and said hello in broken English. He said a few words in English but would finish his conversation in a different language.

One of his friends comes over and says, "he is Italian, and his English is limited." He could keep a conversation if his friend filled in some of the words.

He tells me his name is Sylvester, and I tell him mine.

In his broken English, he says, "I love that name."

He asked me to dance, and I love to dance that we danced most of the night.

My girlfriend came over to see what was happening. I introduce her to Sylvester.

One of his friends comes over, and now the fours of us are making conversation.

We agreed to meet the following Saturday night.

There was something I liked about Sylvester, was it because he reminded me of Chris or his foreign accent.

The web thicknesses

For the next few months, we saw each other quite a bit and became a lot more involved. Then he told me something that I never dream. He wanted me to marry him, now. I asked him, "why so soon we only know each other a few months." Then he told me, "he had jump ship and was here illegally." The only way he could stay was to marry an American citizen.

I was not sure what to do, my parents would never understand especially my father.

Being young and foolish I said, "okay."

We went to city hall to get the marriage license and our blood work done. Once everything got finalized, we were married.

He had to return to Italy and go thru legal channels; which would take a few months.

So, I had time to tell my family but was too afraid.

A few weeks have passed, and one afternoon I was cleaning out my purse. My wedding band fell onto the floor and rolled right into my mother's foot. She looks down and pick it up and shouts out, "what the heck is this?"

"Did you do something stupid?"

"Thank God, your father is not home."

I was speechless.

My brother hears all the commotions and comes into the room saying, "what happened?"

Ask your sister.

I told them I eloped and was trying to find the best way and time to tell everyone.

My brother says, "o-boy wait till dad hear this!"

When father came home, I told him.

I guess he was in shock because for the first few seconds he did not say a word.

Then he shouts, "Are you pregnant?"

"No, father."

"Then we will have the marriage annulled."

"No father I love him!"

He says, "you are too young to know love."

My father shouts, "where is your so-called husband?"

When I told them the whole story, everyone jumps all over me except my one brother.

He came to my defense and spoke his mind.

My father said, "you are getting the marriage annulled, and that's final."

"No father, I must agree with it, and I will not let you control my life."

"If you do not respect my wishes, I want you out of the house."

I said, "fine once I get myself organized."

"No, you will leave now."

My mother shouts back, "come to your senses she cannot live on the street."

Making our move

My mother says, "your father loves you and only wants the best for you." He speaks of anger, and not from his heart."

I understand, "but I did what I felt was in my heart."

I will start looking for an apartment and get it ready, so when he comes home, we will have a place to live. I found a lovely apartment on the upper east side, and my mother even helped me fix it up.

He returned three months from the day he left.

My father came around and asked us to make a parent's wish and get married in our church. We both agreed and were re-married a few months later.

Sylvester worked and went to night school to get his high school diploma and went to college to earn a degree in engineering. After he graduated got a job for a well-known company earning an excellent salary.

We got blessed with five children and six grandchildren and three great-grandchildren.

We celebrated our 50th anniversaries just a few years ago,

I started out young and foolish, but life taught me a lesson.

"Do what your heart feels, and not what others' may say."

Music to my ears

My name is Maria I was born and raised in New York City. We were a family of seven, three older brothers and a sister. Yes, I was the youngest. Our parents came from Greece and were strict on our heritage, even to the extent we only spoke Greek at home.

At an early age, I enjoyed listening to Greek music and stayed with it while I was growing up. I would attend a lot of the Greek dancers and enjoyed the singers and the brands; I especially enjoyed the instrument called the Bouzouki. Call me old fashion.

Trying to please my parents

I would attend dances with my sister and got to meet a lot of Greek fellows. Some of the guys I met were either a lot older or what I called Greece balls (just off the boat) not my taste. If I told my parents, I met a Greek fellow who happened to be a doctor they were ecstatic. Even before I would have got to know them, they ask, "are you going to marry him."

Maybe I was too particular; I could not get to like many that I dated; they were too short or bold, or even to fat. I dated a lot of professional's fellows like doctors, lawyers, engineers but was having no luck, so I just continued to enjoy myself and play the field.

My sister had met a fellow and got married so now I had to go by myself to the dancers.

My luck changes

I enjoyed playing the field, but my father was getting upset by saying, "what are you waiting for?" "Your sister is married and has a family; do you want to be an old maid?" I tell my father I'm only in my late twenty's.

At one of the dancers, while I was talking with my girlfriends the Bouzouki player caught my attention. There was something about him that I just could not pin point.

He had an excellent voice in fact while he was signing, I could sense he was looking at me. When the band took a break, the Bouzouki player came to the bar where I was sitting with my friends.

He walks up to me and says, "you caught my eye, may I buy you a drink." He said his name is George and was doing a performance tour. He told me he was from Greece originally and was in town just for the week.

He lived in Chicago, and travel's the country doing different affairs. We spoke till his break time was up and ask to see him after the dance.

We went out for a few drinks; it was getting late and told him that my father is strict about staying out too late.

He asked for my phone number and took me home.

George called me the next day and made plans to get together before he left.

I did not tell my parents anything, especially my father because he had a bad habit of always pushing marriage.

Things only get better

For almost a year I was seeing George every other weekend wherever he was performing. If was not local I would travel even as far as Savanah Georgia. I would just tell my family I was visiting friends.

My father would remark ever so often about marriage, and would just pamper him.

I was falling in love and was hoping George felt the same.

He came to New York to do a dance/dinner show, and little did I know he was going to surprise me.

When we got there, he had a table reserved. I said, "why so many." No sooner I sat down my whole family shows up. I was surprised, "what are you all doing here?"

My mother says, "George invited us for a special event."

After his performances, George told the crowd he had something to announce. He walks down from the stage with the microphone in his hand and comes to the table. He gets on his one knee and puts this beautiful oval shape diamond ring on my finger and says, "I love you Maria with all my heart, will you be part of my life!" The crowd is going wild with applauses, and whistling; while I'm trying to say yes.

Icing on the cake

What more could I ask for, got my wish, got the man I wanted and my family was here to celebrate this happiest occasion. So many of the crowd came over to congratulate us. It was an evening I'll always remember.

My father threw us an engagement party, in fact, it was at the dance hall where we first met.

Between Georges family and friends not to mention mine we were lucky to find a place to have our wedding reception with the amount of guest.

Being my father was a baker he made us a cake for our wedding that stood taller than I, and I'm five- five.

We spent our honeymoon in Hawaii.

We were blessed with three beautiful daughters and live just outside of Chicago.

Coast to Coast

My name is James; I recently got divorced after two years of heart aching problems. After the divorce, I kept a low profile. I moved to Californian because of my job, and grew to love the area mainly because of the weather; not to mention I loved playing golf and played it all year around.

My family and friends were living on the east coast, so it made it a little harder to see each other.

After a few months, I decided to go to some of the clubs and see what was out there. I would date, but nothing seemed to please me, so I just continue to go to the clubs hoping for my luck to change.

Matchmaker

My family and friends would fly out a few times a year, and I would travel to the east coast on business and holidays during the year.

One of my friend's wife, tells him she has a friend named Paula that also just recently divorced. She went on and said you two would make a great couple. She mentioned me to Paula and seemed to be interested, but just coming out of a divorced herself she was a little reluctant.

I asked, "Where does she live?"

"She lives on the east coast."

"amusing," I say.

Then she told me her age.

When I told some friends one commented, "with your immaturity and her maturity, it works out."

I did a lot of traveling for my job and found out she also traveled.

She gave me her phone number and said, "give her a call."

I hesitated to call, but hearing all the right things about her, I decided what do I have to lose.

Hitting it off

Knowing Paula's busy schedule from my friend's wife, I waited for the weekend to call her; we spoke over an hour and it just so happens she had business on the west coast, and we made plans to meet. We had some things in common she loved to work out and do marathons. We made plans to do a five K marathon for my friend's family in a few months.

Other times we would meet half way cross country and spend weekends together. When she or I were on business, we made it a point to see each other.

She later told me she had a son and was not sure how I would take to it.

I took a real liking to Paula and welcome her child, and hopefully, he would take to me.

The more we saw each other, the more I got to have more affection for her.

We were seeing each other for just about a year, and in that time, we saw each other well over a dozen times.

A new beginning

After being on the west coast for over a dozen years. I was contemplating making a job change. My old boss had left the company and was now working on the east coast. When he learned about my new love in my life, he asks me if I wanted to come east and work under him as we did in the past.

When I told Paula, she was thrilled and happy to hear the news.

As much as I would miss many of the friends I had made, and not to mention the perfect weather. Everything was falling in place and realized it was time to move on. I gave notice, and many of my associates were disappointed; they gave me a nice send-off.

Getting organized

I had to report to the central office in New York City. My new job would have me traveling from Florida up to New Jersey and as far west as Chicago. My parents were still leaving in New York City, so I stayed with them till I got my self-established.

Paula lived south in Georgia near the Florida border. She had a small condo which was too small for the three of us.

Her son was just five years old and was not to thrill when we first met. I guess he felt I was intruding on his father's territory. I kept a positive attitude hoping it would rub off on him. Sometimes I would either drop him off or pick him up from preschool, and we started to bond a little each time.

Being we were both divorced we decided to wait before making that move again.

So, we decided to buy a home not too far away, because she wanted to stay close to her parents.

I found a nice size house about half hour ride from her parents.

We moved in about sixty days later.

Paula loved the house it had everything one would want, including a pool.

Home run

Little Mark was going to celebrate his big six Birthday, so what better way to improve our relationship. I knew it was important to win Mark over I just wanted him to realize I was not trying to fit into his father shoes. I just wanted us to be more than friends. So, I went a little overboard just to make his birthday party that much nicer. The party was huge success and Mark, and I got along even better now. I reminded Mark that I want us to be close.

Mark had joined the little league, and we go to the practices and games when I was home.

Excitement

When I returned from a business trip, Paula told me that we were going to have a baby. I was excited; my concern was my parents not being married I was not sure how they would take to the news.

When I told my parents, they were happy as could be especially my father.

As for her family, they were just as happy. Even little Mark was tickled pink, knowing he would be a big brother.

I wanted to make our life tighter, a little closer, so I decided to take a weekend trip to New York and surprise her with getting engaged. We invited her parents to join us, and for them to meet my parents.

The same day I talk to her father about my intentions, and he welcomes the idea. I told no one else until it was official.

I wanted to do something different like taking a horse, and buggy ride thru central park would be a nice jester when I gave her the ring. Now that her father knew what was going to occur, he said, "just you and Paula go, and we will stay here and wait." Paula was upset her parents were not coming on to the buggy ride; little Mark says I want to go.

I tried to get down on one knee to propose, at the same time I'm reaching into my pocket for the ring. It had fallen so deep in my pocket I had a hard time reaching it. When I ask her for her hand in marriage, she says, "where is the ring?" I finally locate the ring and put it on her figure. She happily says, "yes" and Mark says, "no."

Now Paula realizing why her parents stay behind.

When we returned, she shows her parents the ring, her mother shouts out with excitement, getting everyone attentions.

The next day her parents met mine, and all went well.

We are taking one day at a time, and let time work things out.

War and love

My name is Harold and just graduated High school. I was not planning on going to college so got a full-time job working as a security guard.

I met a girl at our community center, and we were enjoying each other's company.

Soon after Japan attack Pearl Harbor, I received a draft notice. So instead, I decided to join the Navy.

My girlfriend was not too thrilled, and she proves it by sending me a Dear John. She did not waste any time I was even out of basic training. I took it badly at first, but with all that was going on, I just filed it under B, as a bad experience.

After all my basic training, I took a battery of test, to see where I fit. When it all came about I was to serve in security as an S.P, shore patrol. I went for advanced schooling in the art of riot and disaster training. Finally, after eight weeks of non-stop training, I graduated amongst the top ten, out of two hundred.

My first assignment

Being I graduated from the top ten I was put in charge of our group of twenty-five. Our team was sent to Pearl Harbor to help with the restoring of the carnage the Japanese left.

I met this Philippine nurse named Aya; she was on assignment at one of the hospitals damaged during the attack. She resented anything I did, and being in charge we had our quarrels, and many times had to set her straight. She remarks I was just a kid and was still wet behind my ears. I told her we must evacuate due to unsafe structural damaged. She argues that some of the patience's were unable to be moved because of their severe conditions. One of the guys from the team put together this stretcher that could transport the severely injured patients without any danger to their already injured state. Aya at first was not too thrilled, but we assured her it would be alright to move everyone to a safer environment.

Our team with the help of the army engineering core put together a makeshift hospital. Aya would commit on the health conditions of the temporary hospital. I tried to explain this must do for the time being.

A few months had passed, and with the war in full rage, there was always that concern of the Japanese might return. Security was tighter than ever.

Whenever I had some time off I asked Aya to have a drink, she always made an excuse.

Transferred

The Japanese had invaded the Philippine island shortly after the attack on Pearl Harbor. Late 1942 the Japanese's sent more troops which gave the enemy a stronger hold on the Pacific; this brought a strain on our troops causing more deaths and injuries.

A shortage of experienced nurses became serious, Aya and a few other nurses volunteer. Being it was Aya homeland she felt in her heart to go. The other nurse gave them a send-off and wished them all the best. I took a real liken to Aya even though we were always disagreeing; I was going to miss her.

It was not the same her not being here. Some of the nurses would write her, and they told me she would ask how I was.

About a year had passed, and our team was being shipped out, the rumor was the Philippines. We were going to replace another group of SPs that were either killed or seriously injured.

After the attack Pearl Harbor, it was not as bad as other parts of the war. So, in general, it was a piece of cake. We had ten days before we were being shipped out. Just before we left our new replacements arrived from the states. Things were going to change, as they say from the frying pan into the flame.

Getting my feet wet

It was official we were bound for the Philippine island; what part was unknown.

I was just twenty years old and was scared because of the unknown.; and already was planning on a one-way trip.

Just before we left one of Aya's friend had given me a picture of Aya, I kept it my pocket near my heart.

When we arrived, deep down I was nervous. I never realized how many small islands the Philippines had, it was in the hundreds, maybe even in the thousand and most inhabited. The enemy had taken a position on many of the larger islands.

We got kept in the dark as to the name of the island we were on, due to security. Everything was in code. We were sent to the far side of an island to where we got stationed, during our stay. Once we got establish, I was giving exact instructions on our mission and got assigned to a PT boat, where I met the ship's commander.

Our assignment was to patrol the surrounding islands and answer crisis that may arise. The problem we discovered were mines that were planted by the Japanese.

We received an SOS from a location not too far from our post, so we check it out. No sooner we got to the site we got fired upon, and immediately shot back; the problem was we could not see the enemy. The shooting stopped and took precaution mainly because this terrain was new to us. Later when we felt all was safe, we returned to our base.

The commander remarked that they were checking us out.

What were the odds

While we were out on patrol, we got fired on, and many of us were injured and sent to the hospital. I got some scrap metal in my chest. Lucky, I was wearing my helmet because a piece of metal debris was sticking out of my helmet.

As I was coming out of my anesthesia, my eyes were just focusing on my surrounding and see a familiar face. It was just about two years when I last saw Aya.

Her first words were, "How are you feeling?"

I said, "after seeing you I feel great!"

"When I arrived here, you were always on my mind." "God works mysteriously, I wanted desperately to find you, and here you are!"

Things change

I was released from the hospital a few days later, and before checking out, I told Aya I would love to see her again. She agreed, and we made plans to get together.

It was good to get back to my unit and see the guys again. When I told, them

I found my lost love some of the guys would tease him on my relationship with a nurse, especially her being an officer.

She was on a tight schedule, and when I managed some time off she had to work, so it made it difficult to get together.

I wanted so badly to be closer to her. I spoke with my commander about getting transferred to the security section at the hospital. He said that he would try, but don't be disappointed if it does not happen.

A few days later he told me that the transfer was not approved. He said if I wanted I could take a two-week assignment while one of their team men was on a family emergency. I was disappointed but understood after he explained why; on the positive side, I welcomed the temporary assignment. Just knowing I am in the same complex was more than I could ask.

Takeover

Within hours after I got myself settled in the Japanese had launched an attack on the hospital. All I could hear were the sounds of gunfire and screams.

Being in a strange surrounding and with all the commotion I felt helpless. There was no one around, so I got myself situated. All I had was my 45 and one clip for backup.

I cautiously ran over to the hospital looked around. I went room to room looking for survivors and came across some patience and a doctor who was injured. He told me that the Japanese had taken many of the doctors and nurses hostages. All I was thinking now was Aya' was she one of the hostages or one of the casualties. I ran into some of the SP's and told them I was looking for one of the nurses. So, with no luck I kept checking all the rooms, there was no sign of her.

I backtrack where the enemy had entered the hospital hoping to find some clues as to where they may have taken the hostages.

While I was looking, a young Philippine girl says, "Hello GI." She spoke in broken English saying, "I know where they took the doctors and nurses." I immediately contact the SP squad leader and told him what I just learned from the little girl.

He says, "it might be a trap."

"Yes, and maybe not."

I was not taking any chances and contact headquarters and told them the story. They told me to give them the exact location when we got there.

We got our gear and followed the little girl to where she said they were. The girl pointed out the location; we could just about see the tent. It was that well camouflaged. I thanked her with a kiss on the cheek and told her to go back home.

All safe

One of the guys crawls up to the tent to see what we had to do to rescue the hostages. Between the doctors and nurses, there were over a dozen and only four enemy soldiers. We radioed headquarters and gave them the exact locations and the information. The team leader gave us the plan of attack, and we cautiously crawled up to the tent. My job was to take down one of the enemy soldiers when he gave the signal. I took out my knife and got behind this tall but thin soldier, once I got the command took him down. One of the other enemy soldiers managed to get a shot off and hit me in the leg before he was taken down.

With all the commotion, all the hostages ran for cover. The team leader yells out, "it is now safe!"

One of the doctors came up to me and check out my injury. While he was attending, my wound Aya comes over and says, "Not again it seems every time I see you're injured."

"What am I going to do with you?"

I say, "marry me."

We escorted all the hostages back and got the hospital into some running condition.

Conclusion

We were married six months after world war II ended. We both stayed in the service until Aya got pregnant. Later moved to the west coast and had three children, and blessed with four grandchildren and seven great-grandchildren.

Aya recently passed away; I sure miss her!

I just celebrated my ninety-third birthday.

In life, if you want something never give up.

With all I, have experienced during my life; I would never want to change anything.

~~D~~etermination

My name is Camila and was born and raised in Manhattan. I was the only child. If fact I was a change of life baby. My father died when I was young; my mother and I became very close. I was friendly with a Greek girl and hung out together. In fact, we even went to the same grade school and high school.

Years later when we were in our late teens, they tore down the apartments we lived in and moved to different parts of the city. We remain, friends just did not see each other as often.

~~O~~ne never knows

When I was my early twenty's, my friends would tell me that I had become very opinionated and was not afraid to speak my mind. Maybe I was, but that was me.

I just felt when you want something in life you fight for it.

I would go on dates, but many of them were just one-timers.

I got to enjoy horse backing riding and go to Central Park on the weekends. Most of my friends were not into it, so I go solo.

I got to meet a lot of couples and made friends with some of them. I felt kind of strange when they invited me to their house for a drink. Being I was dating no one, I would invite one of the guys that I was friends with at that time.

My Greek friend Marie called to ask me to be in her bridal party. She said the wedding will be around November and would get back to me with all the details. Now, I was curious to know whom my partner would be.

Meeting my match

A few days later Marie called and gave me all the details on the wedding. I immediately ask her, "who is my partner?" She tells me it's Georges first cousin John.

Maria told me a little about him and was excited as could be, and could not wait to meet him.

The day of the rehearsal I had my hair done just to look that much nicer.

I got to the church extra early, and see this guy waiting in front of the church. He says hello, "are you here for the wedding reharls?" I realized it was Georges cousin John, my partner. He was just as I picture him. I introduced myself, and we chit-chat until everyone else showed up.

The wedding went well, and John and I hit it off. I gave him my phone number and said he would call me.

Trying to connect

After waiting over two weeks John never called, did I miss his calls. I had no way of calling him. I did not want to bother Maria, so I called Georges sister who I met at the wedding. I called her and asked her for John's phone number, she did not have it and would get back to me. Was I impatient, I was so caught up with John I wanted to see him again. Now I was wondering why he never got back to me. Georges sister finally called me and gave me John phone number. Without wasting a second I called him, but all I got was a busy signal. For over an hour it was busy. Finally, after numerous attempts, the phone rang. Not wasting a second I said, Hi John, remember me, Camila from the wedding.

He said you would never believe what happen. I left the paper with your phone number in the rented tuxedo pocket, and never realized it until I tried calling you.

John says, "how did you get my number?"

"From your cousin, Marian," I happily said.

Playing hard to get

John seemed a little shy, and he cut me short and said he was on his way out and would call me back. I was a little upset, but I took a liking to him and would just take it one day at a time.

A few days had passed and still no call back from John. I wanted to call him but felt I would be too pushy. I waited a few more days and decided to call him. I used the excuse my phone was not working. When I called him, he seemed almost like he did not want to talk. So, I had to be the one to be forward and make plans. I just said how about having dinner Friday night.

We met at this dinner in his neighborhood; when he greeted me, he shook my hand, and I gave him a kiss on his cheek. After talking, I came to realize we had a lot in common. The only drawback was he was a lot older than I came to realize.

Trying to break the ice

We started seeing each other almost every weekend; we go horseback riding, in fact, he had his horse that he stabled in Brooklyn.

He began to come out his shell and get more talkative.

About six months had passed, and I started giving hints about marriage because knowing John I feel he needed a push in that direction.

I told my friend Maria about getting married, and she brought it up about our age difference. I assured her that was the least of my worries.

It was time to meet our parents; I knew my mom would like John. My mom took a real liken just as I predicted and welcomed John.

His parents were not very happy; I'm sure being a lot younger and Italian did not help. Even his sisters did not take a liken to me.

They were both married, one of they lived the other side of town, and the other just a few blocks away.

I had my work cut out; I loved John and was not going to let anyone break us up. I wanted to know more about his heritage and his family, hoping to bring me closer to his family.

I thought things would change over time; boy was I wrong, the more we saw each other, the worse it got. I could see no matter what I did or said nothing was going to change with his family. I just kept a low key.

Fighting the odds

Almost a year from when we met, we decided to make it official and announce our wedding plans. We had a small engagement party only half of John's family help us celebrate the occasion.

John told me his one sister said I should break it up between us. I told her outright, "to go and jump into the east river."

John also said, "it's my life mind your own business, you're just jealous that

I found someone that truly loves me." I gave John a kiss and realized I made the right choice.

Up until our wedding, even his parents tried to talk him out of getting married.

We were married in his church and had a beautiful wedding, and his whole family was there.

We enjoyed each other's company and did a lot of traveling and even purchased a small chalet in the Poconos mountains.

We celebrate over forty years before John passed away. We had an active and fun life together. I do have just one regret, was not having a family of our own.

Mama's Boy

My name is Tom and lived in Baltimore. It was just my mother and my older brother. Our father had passed away when we were in our teens.

I always relied on my mother; she cooked and washed all my clothing. My brother had gotten married, so he was out of the house.

Being my brother was practicing law, my mother wanted me to be a doctor. My mom wasn't thrilled when I graduated high school and decided to become a police officer.

I was always concern about my mother whenever she when out, and would always phone her just be sure she got home safely.

My brother wanted mom to move down to Florida to be close to our relatives and wanted me to go down with her. I always told him if you are that concern why don't you move with her.

Someone new in my life

Mom got an invited to a wedding and ask me to go with her. I agreed and took out my suit that I haven't worn for years.

While we were, seating having our meal, this girl walks by the table and says, "Hello." I said hello back and asked my mother if she knew her.

She responds, "no and besides what do you want to do with her, she all skin and bones."

I replied mom stop it, "she pretty and has a nice figure."

When the band started playing I ask her to dance. Her name was Gloria, and we danced and chatted a while.

I could see my mother waving, so I asked Gloria for her number and told her I call her in a few days. My mom says, "why are you wasting your time with her; you can get any girl you want."

I called Gloria and ask her if she wanted to get a bite to eat; I took her to the local tavern where I go with my mother many times.

After dinner, I made a phone call. When I returned, Gloria asks me who I phoned. I told her my mother just to be sure she got home all right. She questions me "do you make a habit of calling your mother?" I told Gloria, "I'm just making sure she is okay."

When my mom found out that I was seeing her, she asked, "why in heaven's name are you bothering with that skinny girl." I usually do not argue with my mother, but in this case, I liked Gloria and stood up for her.

Getting more involved

I got to learn more about Gloria; she had lost her mother at a young age. She was the only child and lived with her father. She was a hairdresser for one of the famous stores here in Baltimore.

I invited my mother to dinner to meet Gloria, my mom at first said, "no." I told my mom if you want me to continue living home I suggest you have dinner with us. She argues and eventually changed her tune and joined us for dinner. Mom was hard on Gloria at first.

After talking with Gloria mom seemed to mellow out.

Gloria invited my mother for a Sunday lunch, and she accepted.

My mother says, "maybe I was wrong."

I asked, "what changed your mind."

"Just talking to her."

Came Sunday, we stop to pick up some flowers before going for brunch. I would meet her father for the first time. Her father was quite the man he was easy going and very knowledgeable. I could sense her father took a liking to my mother, but knowing mom, she would have no part. But at least they got along.

One of our cousins was getting engaged, and they invited my mother and me. My mother says to be sure to ask Gloria to join us.

The party was at the tavern that I took Gloria the first time we went out. Everyone was enjoying the party, one could tell from the amount of beer consumed.

As we were leaving my uncle says to my mom, "I'll drive you home." I was a little reluctant because he had his share of drinking.

Mother says, "don't worry I'll be fine."

When we got to Gloria's house, I called home to be sure mom made it home safely.

Making my move

I took Gloria out for her Birthday and ask for her hand in marriage. She said to me, "what about your mother." "You seem always to put her on a pedestal." I assured her that things would change once we are married.

When I told my mom, she was thrilled and threw us an engagement party. We celebrated our engagement party at the tavern with family and friend's not to mention half of my police precinct.

Her father took my mom home, and I took Gloria home.

I called my mom to check up on her, and again she questions me about it.

I replied, "out of habit."

We were planning our wedding early fall and from the looks of it was going to be over two hundred people, no matter how we sliced it down.

Our parents put together a rehearsal party and invited many of our family and friends from out of town. The liquor was pouring like water, and just about everyone was enjoying a superb time.

I took Gloria home, and her father took my mother home.

When we got to her house, I called to make sure mom arrived safely. Gloria blasted me and said, "I can't believe you called to check on your mother on the eve of our wedding." I said, "I'm sorry, but she is my mother."

No show

My brother, the best man, came by, and we left for church. When we got to the church all was well; every seat filled. Came 3 pm the organ music started playing, but no sign of Gloria. We waited a few minutes longer, but still no Gloria.

"My brother says, "did anything happen last night?" I said, "we did have a little understanding last night, but never dream it come to this." I immediately question her father he said, "she asks the bride maids and me to go ahead, she had to work something out."

I took one of the police cars and race over to the house only to find out she was not home. I notice the wedding grown on her bed. I was beside myself when I returned to the church to tell everyone, "there would be no wedding."

Ironing things out

I went to Gloria house, and her father told me, she just left for the airport. He gave me all the information and raced to the airport to where she be leaving.

When I arrived, she was just checking her bags in. I shouted out to her. Gloria says I'm sorry, "I cannot marry someone who puts his mother first."

I apologize, "your right you come first, please give me another chance."

"Why should I believe you," Gloria shouts out.

"Because I'm cutting my ties and sending my mother to Florida to live near our relatives."

"If you still want to go to New York, we can go together."

"What about your job?"

I know a few friends, that can pull some strings.

We drove back to her house and told our parents our intentions.

They said that they were both going to Florida to live.

Once we settle in, we found a lovely apartment in Brooklyn, New York.

Shortly later we decided to have a small wedding by the justice of the peace. Both our parents and a few friends were there to celebrate.

We had three daughters and four grandchildren.

26

Down to the wire

My name is Bob and was raised up in Newark NJ. I lived with my parents and my older sister.

Shortly after World War II ended I got drafted; after completing my training received my orders, I was going to Germany to do my tour of duty.

I was one of the youngest of my platoon and got teased almost always, but I learned to live with it.

I became close to a few of the guys, and one of them was like an older brother.

When we arrived in Germany, we were broken up into groups. Most of the guys I made friends with got transferred to another camp. Now I felt scared, being in a foreign country. I would take one day at a time.

Getting acquainted

After a few weeks, I got myself into a routine and started going to some of the local clubs with a few of the guys from my unit. I was not a drinker, and not knowing any better get myself intoxicated.

The next day my head felt like it was twice its size. I learned to drink in moderation if I wanted to enjoy myself.

The next time I went with the guys one of them got into an argument with one of the natives and all hell broke out that the MP's came and threw us all in the brig. It started to be a habit every time I would go with them into town something always happened.

Someone new in my life

I started going by myself to the clubs; I was starting to feel more confident as time went on. I was sitting sipping my drink and enjoying the show. I was admiring the singer she was wearing this sexy dress which caught everyone attention including mine.

I would go every chance I could just to watch and hear her sing. Every time I went, I would sit a little closer to where she was performing.

This one time, someone taps my shoulder, and to my surprise, it was my friend Tom who was like my brother. We hug each other and spoke about our experience here in Germany.

I told Tom about the singer and said let me introduce you. I laughed and said, "Are you joking."

"No, I met her I a few weeks ago at a party at our unit."

Her name is Brigitte and is a native of Germany and his 23 years old.

Later when she finished her performance, we went backstage to meet her; I never dreamed this would happen.

When he introduced us, I melted; She looked even more beautiful. We chatted a few minutes and told her, "I have been coming every chance just to see you perform." She thanked me with a kiss on my cheek.

Things get more heated up

Now that she knew of me she waves to me while she was singing. I wanted so badly to ask her out but was afraid of being rejected.

This one time while I was sitting she came over to me and said, "may I join you." We chatted a few minutes, and she said, "do you have any plans tonight." I said, "not really." We went to this coffee shop and chatted for a few hours. As much as I wanted to stay longer, I had to get back to camp.

Another night after she finishes performing this fellow goes up to her, and I see he is annoying her. I run over and say, "stop annoying her." He says, "mind your business."

Again, "I say, stop annoying her."

He swings at me, and I fall. I get up, and now we are both fighting. He was a lot bigger than me. As much as I tried to defend myself, he got the best of me.

When the smoke cleared, Brigitte was tending me with a washcloth, and two MP's were questioning me about the incident.

Healing my pride

Brigitte took me to her apartment and continued to tend my bruises. That fellow was an old boyfriend. She goes on and tells me they were dating, and he was cheating on her, and she broke it off. I was not sure what to do, I like Brigitte but her ex I was not certain how to take him on; Just because she washed her hands of him. I could see he was not giving up that easy.

When I got back to my unit, as much as try to hide my bruises everyone made a commit

A total about face

I took one day at a time, only to discover our unit was moving to another location. We were just giving 24 hours- notice; I did not even have a chance to notify Brigitte about the move.

At the crack of dawn, we got into trucks with all our belongings and drove for hours before coming to our new location.

Once we arrived, we were re-assigned to different sections. Much to my surprise, I ran into Tom; we were going to be in the same quarters.

He brought up Brigitte even before I; he was happy to hear we were hitting it off. Unfortunate being so far away it was going to be difficult to see her.

Trying to locate

Finally, after three months I could take a furlough. I ask Tom if he would mind taking a ride with me because he knew the country better and spoke some German.

When we arrived at the club to my disappointment, she had left about a month before. The owner gave me an address in Hamburg, and said when she left, "I'm going home." It was a long shot, but that was all we had to go on.

The roads were treacherous one could still swell the war had left behind. It was a three-hour ride from where we were.

When we arrived, her mother told Tom in German, "she left about two weeks ago." She did not say exactly where but would notify her when she settled in. She gave us a phone number, to call her when Brigitte contacted her.

It was a long ride back to our unit; all I could now was wait and hope she notifies her mother.

Tom called a few times but with no luck. I was scheduled to go back to the states in a few months and was despite to find Bridget.

Just before I was due to leave Tom called and found out she was living in a town just outside of Berlin called Altlandsberg. I ask my sergeant if I could request an emergency leave, I told him the story. He reminded me that I was leaving for the states within 36 hours.

Finding my love

My commanding officer granted my leave and reminded me not to be late; I was on my own Tom was also going home and had much to do himself.

When I arrived, she was not home; I ask a few of her neighbors unfortunately only spoke German, I sure missed Tom now. All I could do was wait and hope I was at the right address.

I went to one of the local clubs to kill some time; while I was at the bar hear a familiar voice, what were the odds I go where Brigitte was performing.

I got up and walk closer to where she was performing. Brigitte spots me from afar waves to me. She starts walking towards me and even before she finishes singing gives me a hug and a kiss.

When she finished, she starts to cry and says, "what happened, how did you find me?" I explained the whole story and told her, "will you marry me, I do want to lose you again." Brigitte remarks, "we cannot get married you are leaving for the States tomorrow."

Tying the knot

I told Brigitte, "we will find a justice of the peace even if it takes all night." I found a cigar wrapper and put it on her finger, and happily say this will have to do for now.

It was nearing midnight, and we came across a small chapel with its lights on. I almost knock the door off its hinges when this older gentleman says, "what is all the commotion."

I explained, the whole story and was very understanding and says, "please come in." It was like a God sent that the minister happened to be there. He notified his wife to be a witness and were married a little after midnight; I was due to ship out at 7 am.

We had the quickest honeymoon on record. I took Brigitte home and told her if all goes well, you should be State-bound hopefully within six months.

When I returned, they were already loading up for our trip back to the states.

I immediately reported and gave my commanding office the wedding certificate. The commanding office remarked you sure cut it to the bone and assured me everything would be taken care of and the paperwork processed.

Waiting

I was back in the good old USA and was reassigned right here at Ft. Dix, where I did my basic and advanced training. Brigitte and I kept in close contact waiting to hear when she would be able to come stateside officially.

When I told my parents, there were mix emotions. I told them to wait till you meet her, then decided.

I found a small apartment not too far from my parents. Now it was the waiting game.

I received confirmation on her arrival date, and she was officially coming. Just about four months from the time I left Germany she arrived here in the States.

We had our long-awaited honeymoon. Once my family met Brigette everyone loved her and welcomed her to the family.

We got blessed with three children and four grandchildren, and three great-grandchildren.

Coffee break

Every morning I had to have my fix, coffee or I was useless for the rest of the day. My name is Dave, and I would stop every morning before going to work at Starbucks.

This one morning this girl in front of me most of forgot her wallet, so I offered to pay. She at first said no thank you, and I insisted. I had a meeting to attend within the next 15 minutes; so, I cut her short. She thanks me and said, "please I will pay you back."

I replied, "don't worry."

Another cup

The next morning, I was getting my coffee, someone shouts "I will pay."

I turn around, and it's the girl from yesterday. I say don't worry, and she insisted; I told the cashier not to worry, and I paid it She got mad at me and said, "I don't take charity." I said, "I do not give charity." Being pressed for time, I just said have a nice day. No sooner I am walking into my entrance of workplace she appears trying to hand the money for the coffee I paid the day before. She hands me the two dollars, and I give it to a Salvation Army volunteer. She shouts, "I thought you said to don't give to charities." "I don't, you did." She got upset, and storms off and I say, "have a nice day."

Surprise drink

I stop after work to have a drink; the bartender says that young lady at the end of the bar just bought you a drink. I look over and see it's her again. She walks over to me with her drink and says we are now even.

You are a tough cookie, now let me buy you a drink. I'm waiting for my boyfriend. Have another while you're waiting, I don't bite.

A half hour goes by, and I say looks like your boyfriend is standing you up, have another drink.

No, I better call him and see where he is; by the way, I don't even know your name. I introduce myself and tells me her name was Stella.

She goes and calls her boyfriend and comes back saying thanks for the drink and starts to leave. I ask her what happen; she says, "he is running late and is not coming."

Have another drink, and I'll take you home. We had a few more drinks, and Stella started to get more talkative. I realized I better take her home before she passes out. I had to hold her from falling, I flag down a taxi, and before I could ask her for her address, she passes out.

Getting to know you

I had no choice but to take her to my place. When we got there, I took her to my bedroom to let her sleep it off. I slept on the couch.

While I was sleeping, I heard her scream and ran to see what happen. She asks, where am I? I explained what happened and she says my boyfriend will never believe me.

I said, "nothing happened."

"Well, where are my clothes?"

"I took them off, so they won't get wrinkled."

"Don't worry I did not peek."

"It's early, and besides, it's Saturday, how about breakfast." She helped make breakfast, and we chatted almost till noon.

Stella said, "I better get going I'll be doing a lot of explaining."

"Let me take you home."

"No, I better go along."

I told her if there is a problem to let me know. I gave her my phone number and told her to call me if for any reason.

Monday morning, while I was getting my coffee Stella, is online. I asked her if everything was all right. She managed to explain, but her boyfriend was distraught with what she told him.

I was beginning to fall for Stella, what seemed to be a nuisance at first was now in my thoughts. Knowing she had a boyfriend did I have a chance or was I wasting my time.

Things change

A few weeks later Stella called me, can I come over.

"I replied, of course;" she sounded distraught.

She told me she had a big argument with her boyfriend and had to talk to someone. She hugged me saying, "what am I going to do." She explained her story and I told her this is something you must work out.

It was all about what happened that night she passed out, he apparently did not believe nothing happened.

I said, "if he loved you he should believe you."

That what love is truth and honesty.

She says, "would you believe me if I told you the story."

"Yes, if you told me I would believe you."

She hugs me saying, "I knew there was something about you I loved."

It was getting late, and I told her I would take her home.

When we got to her apartment, her boyfriend was there. He wasted no time looking to start an argument. She tried to explain, but he would not listen.

He tried to hit her, and I put up my hand and instead hits my hand. I told him to stop, but he continued. He pulls out a knife; I take off my jacket wrap it around my arm. He comes towards me, and I managed to pull the knife out of his hand. He jumps at me, and we are now scuffling. Within minutes the police arrived. Stella had to explain because they handcuff both of us.

Finally, they set me free and arrested her boyfriend. When they did a background check, he had warrants for other crimes.

Pass the cream

We would meet almost every morning for coffee before going to work.

Stella asked me to go with her to see her parents it was her mother's birthday. They lived about a four-hour drive. I told her I loved the idea and was looking forward to going.

That morning I stopped to purchase some flowers before I pick up Stella. We arrived at her parents' house just in time for lunch.

Her mother was as sweet as pie; I could see Stella took after her mother. Her father was a more serious person and came to find out he was a Doctor.

After lunch, her father asks me if I played golf. I play on occasion; he says good we tee off tomorrow at 8 am.

That night we all went to the country club her father belonged for her mother's birthday. I got to meet some other couples that were also there to help celebrate. After we had coffee we danced; I told her your parents are very charming and I'm happy you invited me.

The big question

Her father asks me many questions while we were playing, and I told me that I was going to ask Stella to marry me.

He tells me, "Stella, is his only daughter and I only want the best for her;" she has a fabulous job working for an investment company.

"I see that you both have great careers, in that case, go for it."

As we are driving home, she says, "my parents like you."

I wanted to propose to Stella, but before I did, I wanted her to meet my family. The trouble was mind were on the east coast; when I ask, her she said she loved too but couldn't get away just now.

I wanted to do something different; it all started here at Starbucks the next time we had coffee I would ask for her hand in marriage.

I put the ring on her blueberry muffin, just as she goes to pick it up she hesitates and screams out yes, yes everybody is looking as I put it on her finger.

She gives me a kiss, and everyone is applauding.

A few months later we flew out to see my family; everyone loved Stella.

We were married a year later; our parents met for the first time at the wedding.

Over the years are parents bonded and became close and would travel to see each other.

We had had three sons later in life.

28

Beautiful eyes

My name is Jeff, and it was just my brother and parents. My brother went into business with our dad. Not me I wanted to become a Doctor; something I always dream to do while I was growing up.

Before I graduated high school, I reminded my parents that I was going into the medical field, and be a Doctor.

My parents were ecstatic that I was going to fulfill my childhood dream.

I applied to different schools and got excepted at a few of them.

When I graduated high school, my parents threw me a party to celebrate my high school graduation and starting college.

It was going to be a long, long road before I could put the word doctor in front of my name.

Making my rounds

The years flew by and before I knew it I was getting my doctor's degree. Shortly after I graduate medical school I started my internship; I made friends with some of the physicians and nurses. I began working with a Doctor Manuel, and over time we became close.

We were making our daily rounds, and I spotted this nurse, she had the most beautiful eyes I have ever seen. When I said hello, she ignored me like I was not even there.

A few days later I see her again and could not stop staring at her. I told my associate Doctor Manuel, "I love to get to know her and maybe even marry her."

He laughs and says, "good luck."

Another time when I saw her working at the front desk, I said hello, and again she ignored me. I wasn't giving up that easy and was determined to get to know her.

A short time later, Doctor Manuel and I were having lunch when he spotted a female friend of his sitting a few tables away. As we were leaving, we went to say hello and much to my surprise the nurse with the beautiful eyes was with her. He introduces me, and she introduces her nurse friend Theresa. We chatted a few minutes and the funny part she did not recognize or remember me at all.

Getting acquainted

Now that we knew each other, we started talking and were getting to know more about each other. We talked about our families and told me; she was one out of ten siblings.

I asked her for her phone number, not that it mattered I saw her more here at the hospital. We saw each other, whenever possible when we were both off.

With the long hours, I was putting in for my internship it did not leave much time for socializing. If it weren't for the fact we were in the same hospital, we would hardly see each other.

We finally got a day off at the same time, so that I could meet her family. Meeting her family was like attending a club group. Her parents were down to earth people and took a likely to me.

I now wanted her to meet my parents, and with our work schedule, it was tough. Finally, she got to meet my family, and they immediately took a liken to Theresa.

Whenever we had the same time off, we took advantage of it. God was work in mysterious ways; we met here, and now we are seeing each other almost every day.

I was falling for Theresa and wanted to ask her the big question; I was hoping she felt the same way. There was something I loved about Theresa and not just her eyes. I just could not pin point it.

I told my parents I was going to ask Theresa to marry me and they were ecstatic to hear that.

We got engaged a few months later.

Giving a helping hand

My father was not one for going to the doctors, his theory was, "if he felt okay why bother." It took a while to convince dad, but eventually, he came around. I asked my friend Doctor Manuel to give my father a complete physical. He also suggested that he have a colonoscopy.

All the other test went well, but when it came down to the colonoscopy my father was a nervous wreck to the point he was shaking, but Theresa came to the recuse. She stayed with him holding his hand to comfort him and assured him it that the procedure was a piece of cake.

When he was in the recovery room, she was by his side, and the first thing he saw was Theresa and said, "I defiantly approve of Jeffery choice." She stayed with him until my mother came.

Now I know what I loved about Theresa, "she had a heart of gold!"

Tying the knot and moving on

I was just about finishing my internship, and we started making plans for our wedding.

We were married a few months after I completed my internship.

I started practicing in the hospital where I did my internship and where we first met.

Years later I left the hospital and started my practice.

Over the years, I became close with my patients, and it was like family with some of them.

Today we were blessed with two beautiful daughters and three grandchildren.

Printed in the United States
By Bookmasters